·HOTHEADS·
and HEROES

By the same author:

The Hope of Glory
Wide Horizons
Exit
One Way Street
Dead End

Non-Fiction
Stopping the Clock

·HOTHEADS· and HEROES

-The- BRISTOL RIOTS of 1831

-Peter- MACDONALD

Christopher Davies

Copyright © Peter Macdonald 1986.

Published by
Christopher Davies (Publishers) Ltd.,
P.O. Box 403, Sketty,
Swansea, SA2 9BE.

ISBN 0 7154 0682 5

*Printed in Wales by Dynevor Printing Company,
Rawlings Road, Llandybïe, Dyfed.*

Bound by Geo. Tremewan & Son, Swansea.

Contents

Illustrations

·HOTHEADS·
and HEROES

Prologue

The Whys and Wherefores

The riots which occurred in the city of Bristol in October 1831 were one of the most dramatic episodes in the history of the United Kingdom. They were the manifestation of bitter resentment against an unfair system, a sudden release of frustration by a growing population held down for centuries by the fuedal system and its legacy but becoming more literate and politically aware as time passed. However, during the furious disturbances there was not, as there had been in the French Revolution, a blood lust which called for the death of those who had created the conditions which led to the frenzied outburst; even at the height of the uproar, when men, women and boys were surging around with their emotions inflamed by passion and alcohol, the very people they were protesting against went about their business with very little molestation. Unplanned, chaotic, violent but not vicious the riots started spontaneously as a protest and then got out of hand as the

1

wilder spirits realised that they were unfettered; that there was free liquor and loot to be had but also, and perhaps of more importance to them, that for once in their lives they could say exactly what they thought and do exactly as they pleased.

When it was all over the city centre was a shambles, hundreds of people had been killed by soldiers, fires and falling buildings and a great many more were slowly dying from their wounds. The corporation was disgraced; those who might have done something but had stood aside were shamed, and scapegoats had to be found. The full weight of the law and of government cracked down and exacted punitive penalties; men were hung, transported and imprisoned. But though it took a long time to come to fruition the seed of doubt sown by the events of those two days in the minds of the few who ruled the many brought some reforms, and, with the passage of time, others. Today's democracy is to no small extent due to the words and actions of a few ordinary and uneducated men who made their voices heard in those overcast but exciting days of late Autumn a century and a half ago.

*

Bristol, once known as Bright Stowe, has been the site of human occupation for a very long time. About the year 920 AD Ella was Lord of the Castle, "a great warrior against the Danes who died in the castle of the wounds he had received by his hostilities with that people". Before that, Bristol had been the site of a pagan settlement, and then, on the Downs, of a Roman encampment. In the year 1050 the Warden of the Castle entered into a solemn league against Edward the Confessor for being partial to the French and introducing their language and laws, but not long after that William the Conqueror brought French influence to bear even more strongly by making himself the Lord of Bristol Castle.

In the year 1244 King Henry III ordained that the Burgesses of Bristol, of whom six would be Aldermen — people given higher status by their fellow Councillors as a mark of esteem — should choose a Mayor. In the reign of Edward III Bristol was made "a county of itself". The senior Alderman would be the Recorder, the lawman who dealt with serious offences, and was to be a barrister of at least five years' standing. (William de Colford was the first, elected to that office in 1345.) It was made a City by Henry VIII, who stayed in nearby Thornbury in the year 1534 and after visiting the place in disguise said "This is now but the towne of Bristol, but I will make it the City of Bristol" which he afterwards did, in the thirty-fourth year of his reign. (He may have been slightly influenced by the fact that the Mayor had sent him "ten fat oxon and forty sheep, and for Queen Ann a silver cup with a cover and one hundred marks of gold". The Queen's family name was Boleyn.)

In 1581 their daughter, Queen Elizabeth I, granted the City six more Aldermen and it was divided into twelve wards, "over which were set eleven Aldermen, the Recorder always making the twelfth". In the year 1683 Charles II granted a new Charter, which confirmed the city as a County within itself. The Mayor and Aldermen were to be Justices of the Peace who would punish petty offenders at Sessions four times a year, while the Assizes, at which the Recorder presided, were to be held twice a year.

In the ninth year of the reign of Queen Anne, in 1711, a new City Charter was granted which confirmed that there would be forty-two Burgesses in the Common Council. By that time the city was quite large in population — some 50,000 — but small in size; clustered around the flat area of land where the Rivers Froome

3

and Avon joined and made a natural harbour for sailing ships, sheltered from adverse winds by the hills which rose up to the West. It was a thriving, bustling port, established long before Liverpool and, without a rival on the West coast, fortuitously in a position to benefit from the opening up of the New World. The Castle, which had for centuries been the hub of life in the area, had long since gone: it had fallen into ruin and was finally pulled down in 1655. The Recorder had become the equivalent to a Judge of the King's Bench — a senior law man with great judicial power.

*

To understand what led up to those events in October 1831 it is necessary to know something of the political background in England at the time.

The drain on national resources caused by the Napoleonic Wars had caused a depression which brought about great unemployment and discontent and led to demands for administrative reform. Very few people had the vote and the system of returning Members of Parliament was wholly unjust: small towns had two Members while some cities — for example Birmingham, Manchester and Sheffield — had none. Those few who were alleged to represent the interests of all in fact, human nature being what it is, perpetuated their own.

On the 16th August 1819, at a place called Peterloo near Manchester, 60,000 people attending a rally in favour of Reform were charged by cavalry: about 12 died (nobody at the time was quite sure how many) and about 400 were injured. Though in the early 1820's some improvement in national prosperity lessened the call for radical change the deep-seated unrest and discontent remained. In 1824 trade unions were permitted (they had been outlawed for 25 years) but because of an immediate outbreak of strikes their existence was again controlled by an Act passed in 1825. Consequently, in the later years of the 1820's there was a resurgence of calls for a more democratic system of government.

Quite naturally, the aristocracy who ruled the country opposed Reform but the middle-class generally supported it (because the aristocracy prevented them from achieving a place in society commensurate with their wealth and status) while the lower-classes desperately hoped it would improve their lot. Also people in the cities hoped Reform would lead to better local government; political unions had been formed in a number of English provincial cities, based on the model of the very active one in Birmingham.

In 1829 the Catholic Emancipation Act was passed, thus beginning to end centuries of discrimination and ill-feeling. (Nearly fifty years before, the politician Lord George Gordon had led 60,000 marchers through the streets of London in protest against the granting of greater political freedom to Roman Catholics; it had been necessary to call out troops when prisons and the Bank of England were savagely attacked.) In the same year an organised police force came into existence in the capital, but there were only parish constables and night watchmen in other cities and towns and sometimes nothing at all in the more remote country districts.

If policing was a disorganised and hit-or-miss affair, punishments by the courts were not: savagery was the norm when imposing penalties for transgressing the law. Death was the dire consequence for even minor offences, incarceration in jail the punishment for owing a penny or two. Prisons were filthy, damp dungeons where many people died from malnutrition or disease. If the culprit got away with those options the alternative was transportation to Australia.

The practice of banishing people to the great and largely unpopulated areas at the far ends of the earth had become increasingly popular ever since the first penal settlement was founded at Port Jackson in 1788. Someone else was ostensibly presented with the problem of accommodating and feeding prisoners, though ships and pestilence being what they were a large proportion of the transportees never reached their destination at all, so eliminating the problem entirely. A transported felon who actually reached Australia alive was made to work on construction projects, such as road-making or bridge-building, or put into bondage with a farmer or other employer, most of whom treated their workers like slaves. Though a convict might eventually get a conditional pardon, which freed him from his master, he had to stay in the colony until his sentence had expired, with little chance of finding employment. Even when able to earn money hardly any managed to save enough to afford the fare back to England.

As to the Army, it was, as had always been the custom, neglected in peacetime and continued to recruit, as it always had done, "the scum of the earth", who were officered by gentlemen who still bought their commissions despite the fact that George I had banned the practice more than a hundred years before. To the population, life in the army was considered to be only a little better than being in prison, both from the point of view of the living conditions and the esteem with which it was held in public opinion, but to the gentry there was kudos and profit to be had from being an officer. For a large amount of money a man could buy a colonelcy and the whole regiment that went with it — and then impose lucrative deductions on his soldiers — or, if a young sprite starting at the bottom, a commission. Advancement depended on there being a spare rank, on the availability of personal funds and, in the last resort, on whether those higher up liked the man sufficiently to want him to rise above his present rank. Merit had little to do with it and some units were commanded by incompetent blockheads.

In July 1830 the government in Paris was brought down by La Fayette and the Bourbon monarchy was dismissed. To people trying to escape from out-moded feudal concepts this was another signpost on the road to political change. There was more unrest, and during the winter of 1830–31 agricultural riots in South and East England had to be crushed by troops — including soldiers of the 14th Light Dragoons based in Gloucester. Farm machinery was smashed, barns and ricks were burned and animals were slaughtered. (Labourers were paid nine shillings a week for an eighty-hour week.) Nearly 1,900 men were brought to trial, of whom 19 were hanged, 650 were imprisoned and another 481 were transported.

Everyone was talking about the need for Reform but the Tories were entrenched in positions of power and determined not to give way. They branded the Radicals — that is, anyone who opposed the existing way of life dominated by the privileged few — as "the Unsuccessful, who ascribed to anyone but themselves their failings; the Dissolute, who were averse to law and religion; the Politically Naive, who had little understanding or education; the Envious, the Turbulent, and the Idle, who preferred plunder to toil: in fact the refuse of society!" They believed that monarchs and governments ruled by Divine Right, whereas Whigs, the opposition party, held that Kings and Commons ruled by virtue of a social compact entered into between them and the people.

On the 23rd March 1831 a Bill to reform the system of representation in Parliament was passed by one vote in the Commons but was defeated in the Committee Stage, whereupon the Prime Minister — Earl Grey — resigned and called for a General Election. King William IV consented to dissolve Parliament and thus "protected" the Bill, making him highly popular with the common people. In the election the Whigs, pledged to Reform, defeated the Tories, who had formed the government for almost sixty years and, for the first time since 1774, two whig members were elected in Bristol. (By some anomaly, indicative of the status the city had once held, Bristol had two MPs.)

Under the new Administration the Reform Bill was passed in the Commons but was then, on the 7th October, rejected by the Lords. There was rioting in Derby on that day and two days later a mob in Nottingham succeeded in destroying the Castle, which belonged to the Duke of Newcastle. (It may seem surprising that information about the defeat of the Bill in the Lords reached the provinces as quickly as it did but in those days carrier pigeons were used to send word of important events from the capital to the countryside.) During the next few days a silk mill at Beeston was burned down, for which three men were later hanged, while in London Apsley House, the home of the Duke of Wellington, was assaulted by a mob. The Marquis of Londonderry was attacked on his way to the House of Lords and had to be rescued by cavalry. On the 12th, some 60,000 people (which seems a magically recurring figure in the annals of protest) marched in procession to Saint James' Palace to present a petition to the King, while all over the country bishops, whose vote against Reform had turned the scale against it, became very unpopular. The country was in an uproar, with meetings in favour of Reform being attended by as many as 150,000 people. When, on 20th October, Parliament was suspended, the nation was close to civil war.

1831 had already been a year of great activity in other parts of Europe; a revolt in Poland had been put down by invading Russian troops; Leopold of Saxe-Coburg became the first King of the Belgians but fighting then began between Dutch troops who invaded in protest and the French, who went to the assistance of the newly-created Belgian nation; Austrian troops invaded Italy; Faraday discovered electromagnetic induction, perhaps one of the most far-reaching events of all time, and Charles Darwin began his first voyage on HMS Beagle. However, these things would have had very little impact on day-to-day life. Communications and literacy being what they were, by far the great majority of English people — and still less the Scots, the Irish and the Welsh — would have known nothing about the Continental wars, and cared not at all even if they had. As for Faraday, his work would have been totally incomprehensible, and the idea that someone would one day say that people were descended from the apes would have been greeted with scorn, derision and cries of "Heresy!".

*

The political scene in Bristol mirrored the unrest in the nation but was more intense than in most places, there being a history of bloody-mindedness and protest.

In 1795 a mob had been fired on in the vicinity of the Bristol Bridge by soldiers led by the Mayor and Magistrates: eleven rioters were killed and fifty-one wounded as a result of disturbances caused by opposition to the tolls on the city's bridges. In 1810 the windows of public buildings were smashed by a mob protesting against an unpopular Recorder, Gibbs by name. During elections drunken oafs invariably assaulted the home of the defeated candidate — according to an Under-Sheriff of the times he had never known a contested election in

Bristol when this did not happen — and this despite the fact that "bludgeon men" were hired by the Corporation to keep order. Bristol had only 114 constables and 115 night watchmen for its nineteen parishes and twelve political wards, in which lived more than 100,000 people.

In the first half of the Eighteen Hundreds the city was not what it had been. The Corporation had allowed it to go into a decline by not reacting to the fact that ships were getting bigger and could no longer traverse the difficult Avon channel and enter the narrow dockland waterways; by not seeing that things would never be the same again and that different work would have to be found for the labour force. The Industrial Revolution had started in the Midlands and Northern England but Bristol merchants had been tardy about changing established and still profitable ways. The Burghers had built the so-called Floating Harbour (which diverted the tidal waters of the Avon and by-passed them around the dock area by way of the New Cut) but in 1831, although the port area was still occasionally crowded with a mass of sailing ships, trade had declined considerably. Affairs were complicated by links with, America and the West Indies and the associated slave trade; radicals said the great merchants, from whom most people in the city gained their living, acquired their wealth from blood and the whip, so that not only did the working classes feel the natural envy of the have-nots for the haves, but also a stirred-up contempt for their morality.

The difference in life styles between the haves and the have-nots in the Nineteenth Century is well illustrated by conditions in the Army. A Dragoon received 1s.6d. per day (7·5p) plus 1s.2d. per day subsistence money, out of which he had to feed and accommodate himself and his horse. But all sorts of other deductions had become standard; payments for medical treatment, for food when it was provided during field exercises, for the services of bureaucrats such as the Paymaster-General, for pipe-clay with which to whiten equipment — and anything else unscrupulous colonels could think of, such as clothing, out of which some made as much as £600 a year. Deductions from gross pay left the man with 18 shillings, net, per year! The officers, on the other hand, had to be wealthy to pursue an army career. A commission in the cavalry, for instance, cost £3,225 — in today's money, which is worth less than one-fortieth of what it was in 1831, about £136,000 — while each advancement cost another £85,000. However, to the upper classes such sums were not excessive, or the system would not have been able to flourish as it did.

In Bristol itself the few lived exceedingly well while the many ate meat once a week if they were lucky, and subsisted on bread, pulses and cheap ale — the water was deadly. At a private dinner in the first decade of the century the Mayor had entertained twenty-one guests, including an Admiral and four Army officers, to a dinner at which they consumed 62 bottles of wine. The whole thing cost £2.37p per head, about £100 today. Contrast that with the fact that in 1831 a servant girl, Anne Reynolds, earned a shilling a week (5p) and her victuals for slaving all hours of the day and half the night in a cheap rooming house near Christmas Steps.

In 1830 Bristol Corporation was largely composed of wealthy, Tory, Anglican, West-India merchants who so contrived affairs as to perpetuate their own kind in positions of power. For fifteen years not a single Whig had been made an Alderman, and apart from Charles Pinney, who was to become Mayor and Chief Magistrate in September of 1831, no other Reformer had come within sniffing distance of being Mayor since 1820. (After Pinney it was to be another twenty-one years before a Whig was again elected to the position of first citizen.) "To be wealthy and Tory was to be elected by Divine Right; to be wealthy and a Whig was to be elected as a matter of courtesy". And what was more, many people suspected that the Corporation were dishonest men: although about £40,000 was taken annually in taxes, only around £20,000 was publicly accounted for.

In April 1830 when the Recorder, Sir Charles Wetherell, came to open the Assize he was welcomed by an immense multitude of Bristolians shouting "No Popery! Wetherell for ever!!" on account of the fact that he had made a viciously anti-Catholic speech in the House of Commons. The mob attempted to take the horses from his carriage in order to draw him in triumph through the streets and when persuaded not to spent their surplus energy smashing the windows of houses owned by Catholics and of their chapel in Trenchard Street. Five months later, after the Bourbons were dismissed in France a message of congratulation was sent by the Corporation of Bristol to the citizens of Paris, praising their restraint and the generosity with which they had treated their defeated opponents. The meeting, chaired by Charles Pinney, was of the opinion that the French had ushered in "a new era in the History of Man" but for the starving, disease and lice-ridden people who lived in hovels around the dock area, subsisting by begging from their fellow citizens or mugging drunken sailors, the New Era was a long time coming. The run-down city had thousands of unemployed men and a polyglot population of touchy Welsh and aggressive Irish, who had gravitated there in search of a better life. Generally, people felt more strongly about Reform than in any other place in the United Kingdom. Indeed there had been so much apprehension about the degree of feeling that special measures had been taken to organise a force of constables who were to be led by officers on half pay;

in December 1830 a Colonel Mair had been sent by the Home Office in London to supervise the plans to keep "the scum that rises to the surface when the nation boils" from bubbling out all over the city.

The progress of the Reform Bill through Parliament was watched intensely. In the summer of 1831 the last of several petitions from Bristol in its favour bore 17,000 signatures, about one-sixth of the whole population, but in the Commons Sir Charles Wetherell spoke with contempt about the petitions and said that people were not in favour of Reform — on the contrary, there was a reaction against it and at the most people were apathetic about it. He may have misled himself by being too eager to accept the views of Bristolians whose opinions coincided with his own, such as those of Alderman Daniel, who was convinced that "our admirable form of government, King, Lords and Commons, was, of all political systems planned by human wisdom, the most perfect and complete".

On the 10th, 11th and 12th October there were three Reform rallies in Queen Square, a spacious quadrangle surrounded by elegant and expensive property, all of which were attended by thousands of people and at all of which the Recorder was loudly denounced. His great popularity of the year before was quite forgotten and the anti-clerical feelings which had existed for some time became evident by the fervour with which the two local bishops, Robert Grey in Bristol and George Law, who had the see of Bath and Wells, were castigated for voting against the Bill. At one of the inflammatory rallies a Mr Taunton, referring to the clerics of the Established Church, asked whether the people "should show respect to a magnificent Cathedral by prohibiting the use of brush and shovel less the vermin therein should be disturbed and the filfth removed?" Even earlier, on 21st January 1831, a Mr Bridgers had predicted that before long "a hand would be seen writing on the wall in characters of fire — the volcano would soon burst and the Government would explode in atoms". A Mr Ham had likened England to the caste-ridden society of India, asserting that here the aristocracy were not content with civility but demanded servility. In America things were better ordered, he said: a servant would not allow himself to be called your servant but your help. "The tree of liberty had been planted in France," he continued, "but it had not yet been watered!" a statement which was greeted with prolonged cheering. Even the army entered into the fray: at one of the rallies Captain Hodges, an officer on the staff of the Bristol Army Recruiting District, spoke vehemently in favour of Reform, saying that he would shed the last drop of his blood in the great battle the people had to fight if they were to secure real democracy.

On Monday, 17th October, Captain Claxton, a former lieutenant in the Royal Navy, once one of Mr Pinney's ships captains and now employed by the Corporation to supervise the work of the Corn Exchange, wrote "out of a sense of duty" to the Home Secretary, Lord Melbourne (who was to become Prime Minister from 1835 to 1841) to tell him of an inflamatory speech by a man called Powell which had been made to three thousand people at one of the rallies in Queen Square. In a postscript Claxton said that he had every reason to apprehend mischief when the Recorder arrived to open the Assizes on the 29th of the month. The next day, Claxton chaired a meeting on the decks of two of Pinney's ships, the Earl of Liverpool and the Charles, moored alongside, at which some three hundred sailors were present. The formal resolution called upon the sailors to "pledge themselves to assist the magistrates in putting down rioting" but the meeting was interrupted by a large number of Reformers, who were eventually ordered to leave the ship by Claxton. They did this and adjourned to the quayside, taking a number of the sailors with them. There, John Wesley Hall was elected to the chair and presided over a heated discussion in which Claxton's prediction of a riot was declared to be "monstrous". The crowd then loudly approved a Declaration that "the sailors of this port express their loyal attachment to His Majesty and his Government but will not allow themselves to be made a cat's paw by the Corporation or their paid agents".

On the 19th October the magistrates sent a three-man deputation to urge Recorder Wetherell to postpone his visit in view of the tension in the City. Under-Sheriff Hare and Daniel Burgess, the Mayor's Secretary and City Solicitor, travelled to London, where they met William Fripp, an Alderman who was already there. Together they tried to persuade Sir Charles not to come, or at least to dispense with the usual processional entry into the City. Wetherell, however, was adamant that they should not pander to popular agitation, a view endorsed by Lord Melbourne when they saw him the following day. However, it was agreed that "all proper precautions should be taken" and that some soldiers would be made available during the Recorder's visit.

On the 24th October the Bishop of Bath and Wells consecrated the church of Saint Paul at Bedminster, a mile or so from the city centre. Placards had been printed and distributed around the city asking Reformers to "read, mark and inwardly digest" the contents, which were signed "A Churchman". On his arrival the Bishop met with a noisy reception and saw the crowd holding aloft a banner on which were written the same words as those on the placards: "Receive him with every demonstration of respect which becomes his exalted rank and Late Vote in the House of Lords. Refrain, therefore, from hooting, pelting, groaning, hissing or any other kind of annoyance which may be offensive to the man who has so recently declared himself against the voice of the People". One man shouted that the bishop received £40,000 a year out of the pockets of the poor, and it needed all the concerted efforts of the vergers and churchwardens to get the prelate unharmed into the church and out again. As his carriage swept him away he was pelted with abuse, mud and a few stones. The Bishop, so it is said, wept.

On 25th October, the decision to send soldiers to the city having quickly become known, the Bristol Political Union distributed handbills saying that if the magistracy were unable to preserve the public peace without the support of the military they should resign; and, what was more, that the Recorder should be asked to step down as the best means of preventing riots in the city, and perhaps bloodshed. (Although rumoured to be controlled by the powerful Birmingham Political Union the Bristol one was comprised largely of independent middle-class men of professional status.)

On 26th October two troops of the 14th Light Dragoons (with Captains Gage and Musgrave in command) pitched camp at Clifton, having taken two days to travel from Gloucester, and a troop of the 3rd Dragoon Guards (Captain Warrington) arrived at Keynsham from Trowbridge. The 14th wore blue tunics with orange facings and the 3rd wore red with white facings. In total there were now ninety-three active soldiers available to the senior officer in the city, Lieutenant-Colonel Thomas Brereton, who by virtue of his rank became the officer commanding all the troops allocated by the Home Secretary.

On Thursday 27th October the magistrates had posters distributed around the city calling upon its inhabitants to help them to preserve the peace when the Recorder came to open the Commission of Assize — the so-called Delivery of the Gaol. (This document was signed by Ebenezer Ludlow, the Town Clerk, a barrister at the early age of 28 and now, twenty years on, a man of long service in the city.) The people seemed to be totally unmoved by this appeal, and by another asking for three hundred "respectable" citizens to be sworn in as Special Constables for the occasion. Bristolians remained outraged by Wetherell's statement in the House that they did not care a fig for Reform, and were damned if they were going to assist the very people who had acted for years in their own interests and with no regard for the ratepayers they were supposed to represent. On the day, only a few turned up, and it was necessary to hire whoever would undertake the duty, many of whom belonged to the Political Union. In that evening's paper the enraged editor of the Bristol Mercury was to call them "hireling Tory bludgeon-men", a catch phrase which was quickly taken up. While the compositors were setting up the print the Sheriff and the military officers reconnoitred the route to be taken by the Recorder when he arrived, and made arrangements for the troops to be billeted in livery stables in the centre of the city. (To make way for them the horses already there were peremptorily moved out.)

Friday the 28th was a quiet, if dull day. The old city, once the second most important in the kingdom after London, when its docks had been packed with sailing ships bringing cocoa and tobacco and cotton from America, then going on to West Africa to collect black slaves to take there in exchange, was outwardly peaceful. Talk in the ale houses was mostly about Reform and the now much-hated man who was due to arrive next day to try the sixteen people on capital charges and the dozens of other felons who were incarcerated in the city jails.

All was not gloom of course. Then, as always, people tried to make the best of life and get their pleasures where they could. For the vulgar rabble bull-baiting on Clifton Down occasionally provided some amusement while for those with different tastes Sheridan's "The Rivals" was being performed at the recently renovated, fifty-year old Theatre Royal. Posters outside proclaimed that the next event there would be performances of Rossini's opera "The Barber of Seville". Madame Tussaud had announced that her exhibition of wax figures would stay open for another two weeks. In the banking houses men discussed whether they should put up the money to build a suspension bridge over the Avon to the design of a Mr Brunel, who was thinking about laying a railway from Maidenhead to Bristol and was now living in Clifton, convalescing from the effects of an accident in the tunnel being bored under the Thames by men working for his father. For once, there were many ships at the quaysides, their sails furled loosely at the yards and their hatch covers open to allow the cargoes to be moved on horse-drawn carts to bonded warehouses owned by Messrs Fry, Wills, Harvey and Avery.

The scene was set for a violent, hot-tempered, bloody and chaotic drama, the fury of which no-one foresaw and which would involve as its chief protagonists three very different types of men.

*

Sir Charles Wetherell, aged 61, the Recorder and of necessity the senior Alderman, was supposedly an inhabitant of the city but in fact lived in London. He was a clever lawyer who had twice been the Attorney-General but had been sacked the year before from that office by the Prime Minister, the Duke of Wellington, because of that violent speech he had made against Catholic

18

emancipation. He took a very active part in politics as an MP for Boroughbridge in Yorkshire, a constituency which returned two even though it had an electorate of only forty-eight men — who voted, so it was said, under duress from their landlord the Duke of Newcastle. (If the Reform Bill received the Royal Assent Boroughbridge would cease to return any Members in its own right.)

Wetherell had been described in the London Times as a very learned knight but the Speaker of the House of Commons had once observed that "the only lucid interval Sir Charles had was that between his waistcoat and his breeches," this being a reference to the fact that when he spoke Wetherell unbuttoned his braces and then leapt about with such vehemence that a gap opened up over his corpulent belly. Another contemporary declared that Wetherell was "half mad, and had a course, vulgar mind which delighted in ribaldry and abuse". He was, however, "inflexibly honest and highly honourable". A formal portrait of him shows a man with a North-Country look about him — a long curved nose, pale blue eyes, thinning hair, clean shaven but with side whiskers. In the fashion of the day he had a high-collared shirt, a thick silk stock, an elaborately embroidered waistcoat and a loosely hung jacket with low sleeves. A contemporary print in profile shows a thin-lipped man with a twisting eyebrow. Caricatures, however, depicted a very different type of man: a big-jowled, pot bellied, brash and smug member of the ruling classes.

Charles Pinney, 38, had been Mayor for only 43 days when Wetherell arrived in the city. He was a wealthy merchant with estates in the West Indies founded by Azariah Pinney (1661–1720), who had been banished from England for 10 years by Judge Jeffreys for his part in the Monmouth Rebellion. Perhaps he felt lucky not to have been hanged, as so many were, for he stayed away for most of his remaining thirty-five years, building up a considerable business. In time the West Indies estate was bequeathed to John Pretor who, in order to inherit, had to assume the name of Pinney. He went to Nevis in 1764 and returned to Bristol twenty years later a wealthy man, with a fortune which was to increase greatly as the years passed. His youngest son was Charles, described by someone as a "pecksniff" of a man, a hypocrite in the mould of one of Dicken's characters. Small and weakly as a child, he had grown up slightly deformed, with just a hint of a hunchback; and, so it was said, to be cold-hearted, pious, and evangelical. A professed Reformer he was nevertheless pro-slavery.

Pinney was the only magistrate not to have been elected an Alderman by his fellows. Being much younger than they he was inevitably under their shadow; beholden to them by reason of being inexperienced and in the minority party. Because he lacked firmly-held convictions and was willing to back off when challenged he was regarded as a political trimmer. Already, for example, he had tried to be impartial as Mayor by refusing to support the Reformers, but by so doing had alienated them, making them believe that he had ratted on their cause. He had been away in the West Indies visiting his estates until shortly before the civic elections and was therefore out of touch with affairs; it is even possible that the preliminaries to his election were done without his knowledge while he was abroad and that he returned to find himself on the short-list for Mayor without having agreed to stand.

As befitted his considerable means he lived in a palatial house in Great George Street, off Park Street hill. His portrait shows a little man with wavy dark hair, clean-shaven but with long side-burns which meet his high collar. His silken stock is held in place by a jewelled pin and he wears square, gold-rimmed spectacles. In October he was but recently married: in some splendour he had joined in matrimony seven months before, on the 8th March, Frances (Fanny) Still, from East Knoyle in Wiltshire.

Thomas Brereton was an Irishman who hailed from Ross, in what was then called King's County. He was born in 1782, a year in which very little of any significance happened except that the brothers Montgolfier built the first hot-air balloon in Paris. Now on half pay, he was not fully retired but held the post of Inspecting Field Officer of the Bristol Recruiting District, something of a sinecure given to officers put out to grass pending consignment to the archives. He had enlisted when aged only 16 into the 8th West India Regiment and at a time when most of his military contemporaries had been fighting Napoleon's armies on the European continent had, through no fault of his own, spent his soldiering days in the sunshine, first in the Caribbean but latterly in West Africa and then at the Cape of Good Hope. In 1815 he had been a lieutenant-colonel in the Royal African Corps where, for a time, he had held the appointment of Lieutenant Governor of Senegal and Goree, colonies gained from the French after their defeat in the Napoleonic wars. Transferring to the 49th Regiment of Foot (later to become the Royal Berkshire Regiment and now part of the Queen's) he had seen some action during the Kaffir Wars and had been the Commander Cape Town Garrison before coming to Bristol in 1823. He had thus been in the city for some time, and was known to members of the Corporation and to many of its citizens, especially the retired army Chelsea Pensioners, as they were then called, of whom there were some three thousand in the city.

Brereton had been married twice, and each time had lost a young wife to the plagues and pestilences which swept mankind away in those days before hygeine was thought of (the first public sewer in the world was not to be constructed until 1852, in London) and anti-biotics did not exist. He had married in January 1818 Mrs Margaret Whitmore, the widow of a major and daughter of a planter in the West Indies, but she had died eight months later of a fever, aged 29. Then in 1823 he had married Olivia Ross, 19, the daughter of a Captain Ross of the 81st of Foot, but she, poor soul, died six years later after bearing him two daughters, Catherine, now five, and Mary, three, on whom he lavished a great deal of affection. They lived at Redfield House, Lawrence Hill, on the Bath road about a mile from the city centre, in a large house elegantly embellished with a grand piano and splendid furnishings: mahogany and rosewood tables, sideboards and chairs; cut-glass and gilt-framed paintings. In the grounds of his imposing residence he had a milch cow and a yearling calf, a bay saddle horse for himself and a pony for the girls, and in his carriage sheds a gig (a two-wheeled, light trap) two bigger carriages and a phaeton — a four-wheeled carriage drawn by one or two horses, which he hired from a livery stables when he needed them. He ate good food served on fine china from silver dishes and had more than 400 bottles of wine in his cellar — and several servants to take care of it all. The only blight on the scene was his hepatitis, which lingered and made him liverish.

Brereton's portrait shows him to be young-looking for his age — boyish almost. He was tall, it seems, and had a good head of hair and small-featured, clean-shaven face, with just a hint of petulance about his expression. According to some, his appearance "bore evident marks of the hardships incidental to military life," while others said he had sad eyes. Not surprisingly, perhaps, in view of the premature death of both his young wives.

*

Saturday, 29th October, 1831

The day dawned typical of late Autumn; cool and damp, with overcast skies. The grass in Queen Square was soggy from overnight rain and moisture made the cobblestones in the roads looked as if they had been highly polished. The leaves were falling fast and bare branches sticking up against grey clouds were a reminder that a long winter lay ahead.

At eight o'clock the parish constables and hired Specials assembled near the Exchange, where each man was provided with a short staff taken from the stock of two hundred which were kept in the Council House. The Mayor, who had been up early and had left home at seven o'clock, addressed them, apologising for getting them out of their homes so early and urging that they show the greatest possible forbearance during the next few hours. . . . Then during the morning the soldiers moved into the city and paraded up and down in what was intended to be a deterrent show of force. This, however, probably had the opposite effect, since it was obvious that the small number of troops present would be quite unable to cope with large-scale disturbances in a place which had a hundred thousand inhabitants: the sight of them in their tawdry finery, tarnished after days spent riding in murky weather would have done little to deter anyone. The 3rd Dragoon Guards then went to the New Gaol and the 14th rode to the Cattle Market at Temple Meads where, in a few years time, construction would begin on the terminus of Isambard Kingdom Brunel's Great Western Railway.

In order to fool the public the Recorder had decided to bring his arrival forward by two hours from the usual time of noon, but in the event word quickly got around and crowds of people began to gather in preparation for his arrival. He arrived late and it was 10.30 before, at The Blue Bowl Inn at Totterdown (only half a mile from the city centre, whereas he was usually met two-and-a-half miles out) he transferred from the carriage drawn by four high-stepping greys, which had brought him from Bath, to Sheriff Bengough's coach for the ceremonial ride to The Guildhall. The crowd which had gathered jeered, groaned and hissed, and as he was driven off assailed him with a torrent of abuse, clods of earth and stones. Startled, Sir Charles anxiously enquired about the temper of the mob but was blandly assured by Bengough that he was not in the slightest danger; even if his reception seemed to be stormy every precaution had been taken to ensure his safety.

Escorted by marching constables and a mounted bodyguard of gentlemen who rode beside the doors of the coach the procession entered the city, where, crossing Hill's Bridge, the carriage was pelted with stones. Blood spurted as some of the constables were hit. (The 14th dragoons, quietly sitting astride their horses at the Cattle Market, kept a low profile.) In Temple Street windows were crowded with spectators while on the pavements outside people jostled for a glimpse of the hated man and a chance to wave a fist at him. "The lower order of females in particular, many of them regarded as being of abandoned character" used obscene and violent language, accusing their men of cowardice and want of spirit for not attacking the man they had been railing against for weeks.

Approaching the Bristol Bridge the coachman and the footman sitting beside him saw thousands of people lining the street and leaning out of upper windows. Then, as the coach, with its excited, prancing horses, began to run the gauntlet its occupants and escort were abused and screamed at, especially the constables who were regarded as having sold out to the Corporation. In the High Street one of them was felled by a brickbat and when the coach reached its destination in Broad Street the solemn and formal reception by the Mayor had to be abandoned because of the angry tumult. A stone struck the Under-Sheriff on the head and sent him reeling and it was some time before the Recorder could alight because of the press of people. Eventually, though, he managed to, tried unsuccessfully to address the crowd and then, ducking under a barrage of missiles, hurried into the courthouse.

There, with a ruffled Sir Charles sitting in his judicial place on the bench, the Town Clerk and the Clerk of the Arraigns started to go through the procedures for the opening of the Assize but the place had been thrown open to the public, as was customary, and they, having swarmed in, now kept up such an uproarious clamour that the voices of the officials were inaudible. The Recorder, trying to make himself heard, shouted that if there was further interruption he would commit those concerned for contempt, but the only effect of this lofty legal pronouncement was to raise an even louder din than before. In total confusion the formalities were muddled through and then, as was usual, the Court was adjourned until the following Monday. The representatives of the people gave three loud cheers for the King and, cackling and pushing, fought their way out to rejoin the dense mass outside.

With difficulty the dignatories entered their carriages but this time the Recorder accompanied the Mayor and the City Swordbearer, John Edgar. As they settled in, the carriage jolted forward and the procession began the short drive to the Mansion House along narrow streets packed with more jeering people — except for one small group of upper class men near the Corn Exchange who managed to raise a weak cheer for Sir Charles. So as to ensure a warm reception for him in Queen Square some of the mob dashed along short cuts to reinforce the people already gathering there, while another group unsuccessfully tried to ram the Major's carriage with a pair of handtrucks, intending to upend it.

When the first of the coaches stopped outside the door of the mayoral residence to let the Sheriff alight the others were obliged to tail back along the North side of the square, hemmed in by loudly-shouting, fist-waving, foul-smelling, men, women and barefoot children. The Mayor's coach quickly became a target for stone throwers, who managed to smash one of its brass and crystal lamps. To the sound of shattering glass, which was to continue almost without interruption for the next two days of high drama, the First Citizen, the Sheriffs, the Recorder, the Swordbearer, the Aldermen and the Councillors scrambled into the civic mansion, were escorted upstairs by footmen carrying long wands, and took refuge in the first-floor drawing room, where they sipped Harvey's Bristol Cream sherry and bemoaned the unruly nature and shocking manners of the city's inhabitants. It was now about mid-day.

While the gentlemen did their best to ignore them, the rabble outside grew bigger and more daring. Initially, the number of people actively engaged in shouting and throwing stones had been about fifty, but two or three thousand were standing in the background, either taking no action to rebuke the conduct of those at the front or else actively encouraging them — and progressively adding to their numbers as feelings of rage and derision spread. The constables who had escorted the procession were now deployed along the front and side of the Mansion House, which was on the Northern corner of the square, and took all the abuse and flying missiles while the Justices stayed inside and tried hard to follow the accustomed routine.

This Reception was the first of the traditional preliminaries to the half-yearly trial of felons. When it was over the leading citizens would disperse and rest for a while and then would come the powdering, painting and panting: the pulling on of silken shirts and hose and velvet breeches — or, in the case of their womenfolk, stays, garter-held stockings and brocaded gowns — the pushing of feet into silver-buckled shoes. After riding back to Queen Square in strap-suspended carriages, handed in and out by footmen, they would, at last, partake of the long, multi-course banquet at the silver-and crystal-covered table. Down in the kitchens, they knew from past experience, the cooks would be preparing meats and fowls and fishes and sorbets and savouries, and the wine stewards would be decanting vintage liquids. It was all very civilised.

The last thing the magistrates had in mind was to behave as their fathers had done during the last serious disturbance and lead the constables out to deal with the mob, heralded by pounding drums and whistling fifes to show that they meant business. Their side-whiskered heads nodded as they drawled pleasantries, while outside the foul-mouthed ones started to prise the cobbles out of the roadway. Although at first patient, the constables predictably became incensed, and eventually a group of them over-reacted and ran into the crowd, viciously hauling out suspects and beating them up. Regrettably, apart from the ill-treatment, this resulted in some wrongful arrests, and further alienated those who, to begin with, had come there just out of curiosity. Many of the bystanders further blurred the issue by making comments like "it's a shame — a pack of Tory constables and bludgeon-men beating up innocent people!"

At about one o'clock, with tempers raging, there were cries of "To the Back!", meaning the Welsh Back, a nearby quayside on which were great piles of faggot sticks. Returning armed with these primitive clubs the mob attacked the constables and chased one into the Float, from whence he had to be rescued by a boatman. A fierce hand-to-hand battle ensued, but for the time being the strong arm of the law prevailed: the rioters were forced to run off, leaving sticks littering the square and a number of men and boys lying on the grass holding their broken heads. As people drew breath the injured were helped away, some of them to the infirmary, and people drifted off, tired and hungry. (No doubt the nearest inn, the Llandoger Trow, the Flat Bottomed Barge, on Welsh Back, did a roaring trade.) It was during this period of relative calm that some members of the Corporation made good their departure from the Mansion House, though Pinney and one or two others stayed on with the Recorder, who was to be a guest there. (The Mayor had already taken the precaution of arranging for his wife Fanny and her mother to go to an hotel in Clifton so as to be out of harm's way.)

At about three o'clock, some of the rioters heard that the prisoners taken earlier were being sent off to the Bridewell jail. They caught up with them in Nelson Street, knocked the constables to the ground, kicking one on the head and seriously injuring him, and released all the prisoners. At about 4 pm, refreshed and intoxicated, the mob reassembled, and began again to pelt the Mansion House. Due to a bad error of judgement most of the constables had been told to go off for a break and report back in the evening. In the face of a prolonged battering by the rioters those who remained (less than a hundred) retreated into the building but managed to repel the mob, who were yelling "Give us the bloody Recorder, we'll murder him!" — while in the background the crowd was singing "God save the King"!

It was then that one of the chief constables advised the Mayor to call in the troops, who had by now moved into Leigh's Horse Bazaar (in the yard of the Boar's Head Inn) and Fisher's Horse Repository in Park Street, both of them close to the Army Recruiting Office at Number 9, College Green. But when Pinney tried to persuade his fellow magistrates that the time had indeed come to use military force to disperse the crowd he was told that as Chief Magistrate it was his sole responsibility! He countered by saying that he had always acted in council, that they should hold a council now and that if they did, and decided to call in the soldiers, then he would do so. The Recorder, his head thrust forward, his hands thrust deep into his pockets and "his breeches partly down", intervened to say that there were insufficient grounds to warrant summoning soldiers. However, something clearly had to be done and the Mayor at last rose to the occasion.

Accompanied by several Aldermen, Pinney went downstairs and outside to address the crowd who, taken aback by his sudden appearance, fell into a sullen silence. After warning the people of the impropriety of their conduct, and urging them to disperse quietly, Pinney was given three cheers! But for all that the undercurrent of dislike and discontent soon bubbled up and some people again started to shout their disapproval and throw stones. Pinney quickly withdrew, but after a short pause, at just before 5 o'clock, reappeared, climbed on to a chair and read the Riot Act. Only a few people could have heard him above the din but those who did took no notice. Under a hail of missiles Burges his secretary was hit on the head and in the stomach and he and His Worship once more beat a retreat. Ten minutes before, Burges had agreed that there was no need to summon the military; after that treatment no doubt his attitude changed. At last Pinney sent for the soldiers.

The mob, their passions inflamed past all reasoning, now launched an all-out attack on the Mansion House. Wrenching the shutters off the windows and smashing down the heavy door they burst in and began systematically to destroy everything they could lay their hands on. Every article of furniture on the ground floor was smashed — mirrors, glass, porcelain, chairs, tables, pictures, side-boards. The low brick wall outside was pushed over and broken up to provide more missiles and its railings were torn apart for use as iron clubs. Urchins climbed up into trees in the square, tore off boughs and hurled them down to waiting men, who broke them up and went off brandishing them as cudgels. Then a group of men and boys brought straw and other inflammable things into the building, built a bonfire in the dining-room and soaked it in turpentine. There were cries of "A light, a light!" but since there was no-one present wealthy enough to possess a flint-box someone was sent off at the double to acquire a means of setting fire to it. Terrified, the kitchen staff fled, leaving meats turning on spits in front of the grates, and kettles and saucepans boiling on the stoves. The constables, however, rallied, and managed to evict the arsonists and stop the other intruders from getting upstairs, where the Mayor, the Recorder and the remaining notables began to barricade the upper windows and doors with chairs, chests and tables. The Mayoral bed was upended and used to block a window while outside, the crowd, hearing that the soldiers were on their way, hurriedly started to build a barricade to prevent them from entering the square.

It was at about this time that Wetherell was persuaded that discretion was the better part of valour and that it would be in everyone's interests if he made himself scarce. Regrettably that evening's banquet was clearly a non-starter, and so was the Sunday service at which prayers for the Recorder and his work were to have been offered up in the Cathedral. In company with Charles Gardener, the captain of a merchantman and a special constable, the Recorder climbed out of an upstairs window, over the roof of the dining-room, down on to a stable and thence over a wall into the back alley. Hatless and unrecognised in the clothes he had requisitioned en route from a postillion, and having thoughtfully decreed that he would be addressed by his companions as a common person, he made his way to Gardener's house in Kingsdown.

Not long after he left, Major Digby Mackworth arrived on the scene in civilian clothes, had no difficulty, it seems, in entering the Mansion House and made himself known to the Mayor. Mackworth was aide-de-camp to the Army Commander-in-Chief and had been visiting friends in Clifton when he heard of the prospects of a riot and decided to stay to "render any little service" in his power to the authorities. Forty-two years of age, he was a soldier of considerable experience who had joined the 7th Fusiliers (later the Royal Fusiliers, now part of the Royal Regiment of Fusiliers) when he was eighteen, carried the Colours at the battle of Talavera in the Peninsular War, and later served in the 13th Light Dragoons (now the 13th/15th the Queens Royal Lancers) and had then spent twenty years in the Ordnance department. Now, shouldering his way past the constables in the hall and on the stairs, he came to the conclusion that "there was a total want of organisation", and that the constables were seriously obstructing things by cramming into the house — though where he thought they should have been he did not divulge. After some discussion of events he joined the remaining Corporation worthies in hanging about waiting for developments, though more Aldermen sneaked out and made their way home as the evening progressed. Many of them lived outside the city and having reached their homes stayed there until the rioting ended and it was safe to venture out into the streets.

When, at around six pm. a contingent of cavalry, (a troop of the 3rd and another of the 14th) with Lieutenant-Colonel Brereton at their head, responded to the summons, brushed aside the barricade and trotted into the square they were enthusiastically greeted by the swarming crowd with loud cheers! A lad standing on the equestrian statue of William of Orange capered about, while below him men waved the tapering top hats, tall and shiny or flattened and battered, which were then the fashion and were worn by all classes. Tom Brereton responded by taking off his hat and cheering too — as did Captain Warrington and his 3rd Dragoons — then, leaving his soldiers sitting with their hands on the pommels of their saddles, he dismounted and went inside to tell the Mayor in his soft Irish accent that the people were good natured and that he was fully confident he could persuade them to withdraw. Pinney nodded and urged him to do just that. The colonel went downstairs, ordered the troops to go in amongst the people and try to "walk them away" — but on no account to open fire or draw their sabres — and himself mounted and rode quietly into the crowd, holding the reins in his left hand. Some men and women reached up to take hold of his right hand and now and again he bent down and shook the hands of those he knew, but while he did his best to pacify them and persuade them to go home his dragoons had great difficulty in controlling their mounts. Frightened by the noise and bustle the animals bumped into people and stepped on them. Fighting them off, men started to prod the horses with sticks, and to throw stones at them. In confusion the soldiers and the mob surged around the square while, in what turned out to be a foolish enterprise, some troopers of the 14th tried to clear an alleyway: met with a barrage of missiles, and unable to get more than one horse at a time into the alley, they had to retreat.

Though his soldiers were now being much harrassed by the crowd the colonel was loathe to use firearms or swords on them. According to Army Regulations troops could quell riots even if a magistrate were not present, and even if the Riot Act had not been read, but preferably they should be under the legal protection of both. Obviously if they were not, and acted on their own initiative, even with the very best intentions, then a judgement as to whether they had acted properly or exceeded their powers would be a matter of opinion, on which an officer's career, and even the possibility of conviction and death or imprisonment on a murder charge, might hinge. It is not surprising that officers were very unwilling, unless they had written authority, to cause death and injury in the suppression of rioting if by doing so they risked being put on trial. Perhaps Brereton was aware, too, that in September 1793 the militia had been called out to quell a riot, had fired on a mob surging across the Bristol Bridge into the centre of the city, had killed eleven people and wounded more than fifty and had then been required to explain their conduct at an official enquiry! Today, the Riot Act had been read and there were magistrates looking down out of the windows of the Mansion House but Tom Brereton did not have that very necessary piece of paper in his pocket. And, besides, he did not want to hurt people, some of whom he knew and with many of whom he had a lot of sympathy. And he believed, wrongly as it turned out, that they would respond to the good sense of his appeals.

The long winter night had begun and it was becoming very cold and damp under the muted glow of the gas lamps which had been lit. The crowd muttered, stamped their feet, thrust their hands into the pockets of their coats or smock frocks or blew on them. At nine o'clock Thomas Sheppard, a corn merchant who lived three doors down from the Mansion House, suggested to the Mayor that the constables should be reorganised into groups and put on guard, with soldiers, around the building. This was done with some success — which was later claimed by Major Mackworth — but the state of mind of the troopers may be judged from the fact that when Sheppard, in command of twenty-five men, was standing behind the Mansion House a squad of dragoons galloped away, and when he asked where they were going was told by the sergeant in charge that they "were not staying there to be murdered!" However, nine men taken prisoner earlier in the day were safely put away in the Bridewell jail.

From time to time Brereton went into the Mansion House to report to Pinney, telling him that the people were dispersing. "If you take my advice," he said, "you will leave them alone. It is getting late and if you don't disturb them they will go home to bed." But to prove him wrong at about ten-thirty two badly hurt troopers were carried in and laid on the floor of the drawing-room, and also a young officer, who was in agony from his horse having fallen under him. (A constable with a severe head wound was already laid out on the dining-room table downstairs.) The sight of the two troopers caused Town Clerk "Sergeant" Ludlow to rebuke Brereton: "Does that look as if the crowd are good humoured?" he asked scathingly. Seeing that the colonel looked very taken aback Ludlow then asked him if he had any secret instructions from the Home Secretary or the Army Commander-in-Chief in the Horse Guards which prevented him from doing what the magistrates told him to do. When Brereton said he had not, was there to execute the instructions of the civil authorities but would like an explicit order, Ludlow retorted, in front of Pinney, and several Aldermen: "Well then, your orders are to clear the streets and get the city quiet as soon as possible." Brereton was still unconvinced and said: "The responsibility is with you. I protest against the use of force. It is not necessary, and contrary to my opinion," but for all that, faced by men who knew what should be done but were not prepared to back their judgement by giving him the written orders he needed, he marched stiffly out of the room and clattered down the stairs with his spurs jingling. Outside, he mounted his horse and ordered the dragoons to draw their sabres and charge the crowd but to use only the flat of their blades on them. As they prepared to do this one of the Aldermen read the Riot Act again — at the side entrance to the Mansion House.

Wheeling about, the troops formed into line and then plunged into the scattering mob. Leaving some of their number bleeding on the ground and others as prisoners the people fled, and by about half-past eleven the square was quiet and almost deserted; only a hard core of inebriated troublemakers continued to stone the soldiers from side-streets, alleyways and the decks of ships and barges moored at the quaysides, where they could not be reached by the mounted troopers. Captain Gage of the 14th went into the Mansion House and asked the Mayor for permission to use carbines on the men in the boats but the idea was vetoed. By then Recorder Wetherell too had flown; earlier that evening he had strolled unrecognised and untouched around the city observing what was going on, but at about ten, seeing that there were no signs of the disturbances ending, he took a post-chaise and went, via the ferry at Aust, across the River Severn to Newport.

At midnight all was relatively quiet around Queen Square but in the centre of the city the ale houses had disgorged their no longer thirsty but still mightily disgruntled occupants, who made straight for the nearest civic building. Hundreds of them attacked the Council House in Corn Street, in which lurked Thomas Garrard, the city Chamberlain, and thirty-five cudgel-carrying civilians who were the only people who had responded to the magistrates' appeal for all right-minded citizens to rally to their aid. With broken glass from more than a hundred panes showering in on them, and expecting every minute that the mob would overwhelm them, they were saved by the arrival of the cavalry in the proverbial nick of time.

Hearing of the disturbance Brereton had diverted Captain Gage's troop of the 14th from the square, where they were being relieved by Captain Musgrave's, to restore order. Arriving on the scene Gage sized up the situation, found it to be "very violent" and with no hesitation at all ordered his men to charge. The mob scattered in front of the cleaving sabres and were chased up the passageways that led off Broad Street and Wine Street. At the head of one of them, the Pithay, Gage drew his pistol to shoot a man who repeatedly emerged out of an alley, threw a stone and then ducked back again; his pistol flashed in the pan, but a soldier at his side fired and brought the man down. His name was Stephen Bush, he came from St George's parish and he was in his Twenties. With his chest blown open he died within minutes. (According to a later report in The Bristol Gazette he was an innocent man who had come up the Pithay out of curiosity and had nothing to do with the rioting.) Another man, Daniel James, who was said to be walking home from work, had his head split open by a sabre in the High Street and died later in the infirmary.

By one o'clock the centre of the city was quiet. At last the people had succumbed to exhaustion and shuffled off to their hovels. Most of the lower classes who had been the ringleaders in the troubles lived nearby, in the parishes of St Philips, St Pauls and St Mary Redcliffe, and did not have far to go. When Major Mackworth left Queen Square at about two in the morning to make his way to the upper-class bastion of Clifton all was quiet. He thought the worst was over, but it was hardly the beginning.

*

Sunday, 30th October, 1831

Charles Pinney had a bad night, as did quite a few people. Some were hurting from cuts or contusions, some were nursing sore heads — in more ways than one. Others, like Brereton, were very worried men.

Pinney and Burges, and two Aldermen, Goldney and George, who alone remained out of the many civic dignatories who had run the gauntlet of the crowd in order to drink wine provided by courtesy of the citizens of Bristol, had dozed uncomfortably on drawing-room chairs, not assisted in their attempts to sleep by the fact that carpenters had been at work all night boarding up the windows and doors of the Mansion House. When, at dawn, they looked out at the clammy light of day the square was sopping with mist and the picket of the 14th Light Dragoons looked thoroughly miserable on their mud-spattered horses. Though the guard had been changed every two hours during the night men and beasts were weary: there had been a shortage of fodder for the horses, which had irritated the men, and their own quarters had been the same as their animals': they too had dossed down in the stables. Now, unshaven and bleary eyed, the troopers took a very jaundiced view of their situation. However, all was quiet, which was something.

At around 5 o'clock Pinney sat down and wrote a letter to his sister in Bath, telling her that he was well and that he had "forebore ordering the troops to fire" during the disturbances. However "men could not stand being knocked off their horses and in one place I fear a man has been shot". Sir Charles Wetherell, he said, had escaped over the roof and gone to London.

At about six o'clock the carpenters finished their business and tottered off home, as did the elderly Mr Goldney, who shared a carriage with Burges up to Clifton, while Mr George went off on foot. At seven, Major Mackworth reappeared, bright and shiny, and reported to Pinney. As they talked they heard the now-familiar sound of stones hitting the front of the building and looking out were horrified to see that the square was again full of people — and, furthermore, that all the soldiers had gone: only a few constables remained between them and the rejuvenated mob. Mackworth immediately persuaded the Mayor that there was nothing for it but flight, an opinion much reinforced by the sound of the newly-barricaded door downstairs being smashed open.

Together, they, a Sheriff and one or two others, the senior constables among them, got out of a back window, dropped to the ground, climbed a ladder to get over a wall and entered the next-door house. There they all made their way up into the loft and, by walking along the roof space shared by the row of houses on the North side of the square, managed to descend into the Custom House. Unobserved they emerged into a back alley and managed to get away. Subsequently, it was reported that the Mayor had been aided in his escape "by a very fat woman in red petticoats," who had been seen helping him over a wall. Many scurrilous cartoons were published depicting the Mayor being given a "leg up" by a monstrously large and blowsy female during his flight but the truth of the matter was never to be satisfactorily established.

Be that as it may, Pinney and company reached College Green safely while the mob made hay at the Mansion House. Furniture was heaved down the stairs and taken outside, the cellars were again broached and nearly five thousand bottles of vintage wine were handed out to the waiting crowd, as well as a large barrel of liquor. It was not long before Queen Square became the site of a Bacchanalia. Dispensing with such niceties as corkscrews people knocked the necks off bottles and upended wine into their mouths. Some staggered around in all directions before they succumbed to stupor, others swilled until they dropped dead-drunk to the ground where they stood, while those who had their eyes on the finery being brought out into the street or hurled out of the windows took a swig or two but made plunder their first priority. Like a bursting boil the drunken mob spurted out of the square into the city, spreading the good news that there was free booze and rich pickings to be had in plenty.

On College Green Pinney confronted Brereton and demanded to know why the troops had been withdrawn from the Mansion House. The colonel replied that they and their horses were tired out and needed rest, he had thought the troubles were over, and anyway their presence was provocative. Peevishly told to get his men back to the square, Brereton mounted his horse and led away some of the red-coated 3rd Dragoon Guards while Pinney, and some Aldermen he had met on the Green, walked down the hill between the horses. As before, the arrival of the soldiers brought forth drunken cheers and shouts of "Reform" but certainly did not deter the mob from what they were doing; and nor did the fact that the Riot Act was again read three times: as on the previous day, nobody took any notice. Brereton was told to disperse the crowd and, as on the previous day, relied on his powers of persuasion to do the trick. While he did his rounds trying to make himself heard Pinney and company retreated first and briefly to the Mansion House and then to the Guildhall, passing on their way Captain Gage and his blue-coated 14th Light Dragoons, who had been sent for to reinforce the 3rd.

When the 14th arrived, the sight of them infuriated the crowd beyond belief, news of the fact that they had caused the death of two men the previous night, and had been involved in putting down the agricultural riots in Hampshire the year before, having flashed around. Men hissed and whistled and then grabbed for the soldiers to try to unhorse them, shouting "Bring them down!!" and "The Reds for ever, down with the Bloody Blues!!" while women screamed a torrent of abuse and threatened to do unmentionable things to the startled troopers. Seeing what was happening Brereton told Captain Gage to withdraw his men, saying that their presence was the cause of the disturbance. Obeying his orders, Gage and the troop began to return to the Green, pursued all the way by stone-throwing hooligans. At the Hole-in-the-Wall public house, and again at the offices of the Steam Packet, the cavalry turned to face their tormentors. Twice the crowd fled. The third time Gage told his men to draw their firearms. Again the crowd scattered, but then, thinking the captain was bluffing, made a rush. They were wrong, he was not. In front of the startled gaze of many well-dressed citizens making their way to morning service in Saint Augustine's church and the cathedral, where the 67-year-old bishop was rehearsing his sermon, the soldiers fired. One man dropped dead and two others were hit. A stray bullet narrowly missed Ebenezer Ludlow's head and buried itself in the church door.

Seeing what had happened (he had accompanied the troop up the hill) Brereton, decisive even if misguided, ordered the troopers to their stables, and returned to tell the mob that he would withdraw the 14th from Bristol altogether, and promise no more shooting, if they would disperse. This pronouncement was again greeted with ringing cheers whereupon, doffing his hat, he is alleged to have said: "I'm for Reform, my boys, as well as you". Though his sentiments took no account of the temper of some of those standing there, or the state of inebriation of many of the rest, his optimism was boundless. As he went off to the Guildhall to ask permission to withdraw the Light Dragoons someone climbed on to the statue in the square and tied a tricolour flag to it on the end of a long pole. More cheers greeted this display of the "Cap of Liberty".

The Mayor and the other magistrates were surprised to hear the colonel's request and were unwilling to agree with it but, as usual, there was no-one there with enough confidence to speak out and take the others with him, least of all Charles Pinney, who, as ever, was unprepared to take any decision on his own. Perhaps, as before and since, the Mayor had been appointed for political reasons; not because of his ability but because he was the least objectionable to the rest of the Common Council. Never having expected to have to show leadership, when the need arose Pinney did not. Though he had shown some personal fortitude the day before he clearly cut little ice with his fellow Councillors while, contrary to what might be expected, in view of his conciliatory attitude so far during the rioting, Brereton was a man who commanded attention, if not conviction. Certainly he had consistently maintained his own point of view. Or perhaps the fact that a retired major-general,

Thomas Pearson, was present and agreed with Brereton's assessment of the situation, influenced matters. Whatever the reason, the outcome was that Brereton got his way: reluctantly, the magistrates agreed that the 14th should leave, provided they were kept "within easy reach". Now there would be only 33 young soldiers and the lieutenant-colonel and his small staff of recruiters left to safeguard the city.

Feeling that perhaps they had overdone things, and urged by Brereton to send for reinforcements, Pinney, during the next few hours, signed urgent requisitions asking for yeomanry and regular troops to come to Bristol from Cardiff, Tetbury, Gloucester and Bath. In seven Post Office "expresses", hired at the enormous cost of £75, his messengers scattered over the countryside as quickly as they could, desperately asking for belated help. Pinney told those he appealed to that his city was in the greatest state of riot and tumult, but in 1831 it took a long time to respond to an urgent appeal. It would be hours, if not days, before anyone arrived to help.

Having made these momentous decisions the magistrates set about quelling the disturbance by distributing posters around the city telling' the inhabitants that the Recorder was Gone, the Delivery of the Gaol had been Abandoned, the Riot Act had been read Three Times and would they all kindly stop Disturbing the Peace and go home. Unsure that their appeals would be heeded the lawmen also asked their fellow citizens to assemble at the Guildhall at 3 pm to assist in maintaining order. One bill-poster had his posters rubbed in his face and his paste-pot jammed over his head, the other ran for his life.

Up at the livery stables the colonel, accompanied by the major-general, told Gage to take his men away. When Gage seemed to be taking his time — he had only sent for his horse, which was elsewhere — Brereton said "For God's sake, Gage, get out of town!" When asked where he should go he was told "Anywhere you please". For want of a better place the 14th made their bedraggled way to Keynsham. It seems that that place was suggested by an ostler who was standing there: his words fell into a vacuum and were seized upon. Harried by the hooting mob, who were still hanging about outside the stables and threatening to burn them down, then pursued up Limekiln Lane — where they had to open fire again when some of the crowd rushed a trooper whose horse had fallen — the Light Dragoons departed with their tails between their legs. It was nearly lunch time.

Charles Pinney went over to the White Lion Inn, where his clerk Burges had reserved a room, changed out of court dress (velvet jacket, waistcoat and knee-breeches, jabot, black silk stockings and silver-buckled shoes) and sent for someone to shave him before he took a rest. Down at the Bridewell House of Correction at the bottom of the Pithay the Governor, Tom Evans, sat having his Sunday dinner. Suddenly there was a hammering at the gate, shouts and a cry of "Hit the old bugger's head off!" Grabbing three swords he gave one to Taskmaster Boyse and another to Stone the Turnkey. The three of them then rushed out into the paved court in front of the house and managed to force the invaders out of the gate and drop the iron bar, but as reinforcements arrived and pressure on the gate increased the bar gave way and the great oak doors crashed open. While the mob ripped them off their hinges and threw them into the River Froome, Evans and his staff managed to get into his house, where the governor took hold of a blunderbuss and pointed it at the sixty or seventy people, many of them women and girls, who were standing in the rain outside his window. Unperturbed by the brandishing of this latest example of modern technology they demanded the keys, in order to release the prisoners taken the night before. Though he held them off for nearly half an hour in the end, with sledgehammers raised against him — which had been stolen from a smithy in Nelson Street — and under a hail of bricks which the crowd found lying conveniently in front of a half-built house in Bridewell Street, Evans had to give in. While his wife, her servant girl, a passing woman who had taken refuge from the mob, Boyce, Stone and his family escaped, the Governor watched the mob turn on the jail, release all its prisoners and then set fire to the chapel. After about an hour flames started to appear in other parts of the prison and, just in time, he made his own exit before the rioters decided to loot his house and set fire to it too.

Smoke from the Bridewell rose above the rooftops of the city as the rioters, drawing more people to their ranks as they went, made their way South to the New Gaol which stood beside the Cut. By the time the crowd had reached Clare Street, only a short distance from the Bridewell, five or six hundred people had decided to join in the fun. Most of them were around twenty years of age and all of them were, according to a Unitarian minister who watched the draggled column swarm past him, "the dregs of the city". A few hundred yards on, the crowd had grown enormously in size. Some of them broke into a workshop and armed themselves with two dozen sledgehammers, as many crowbars and a quantity of iron wedges, all done under the supervision of a "respectably dressed man, short and rather stout, wearing a brown suit and a double-frilled shirt with three pearl buttons".

At the Guildhall, to which Mayor Pinney had been urgently recalled when news came of the attack on the prison, the magistrates could think of nothing to do. When the Governor of the New Gaol (built only eleven

The Quay, with the Tower of St. Stephen's.
Engraving.   C. Mottram, c. 1820.

Bristol from Clifton Wood. Painting. William Muller, c. 1835.
(Courtesy of the City of Bristol Museum & Art Gallery).

Queen Square, 30th October, 1831.   Lithograph.   R. Cartwright, 1831.

Sir Charles
WETHERELL
LEFT
BRISTOL
At 12 o'Clock last
Night.

'OUNCIL-HOUSE, SUNDAY, October 30, 1831.

MILLS & SON, PRINTERS, GAZETTE OFFICE, STEPHEN-STREET, BRISTOL.

Poster: 'Sir Charles Wetherell', 1831.

Cartoon: 'Escape of the Mayor of Bristol'.

Portrait: 'Sir Charles Wetherell'.   Moore, c. 1830.

Caricature of Colonel Brereton.

Portrait of Charles Pinney.
(Courtesy of the City of Bristol Museum & Art Gallery).

years before "at great expense") arrived to ask for instructions they told him to use his own discretion, since they would give him no direction on the matter. Billy Humphries did, and went forth full of wrath intent on turning the mob away from his jail. However, when he and a few citizens who had responded to the magistrates' call for help got there they found their way barred by more than a thousand people, the nearest of whom turned on them and drove them away with stones and hammer blows. Mr Little, an attorney, was so badly hurt by the smashing impact of a sledgehammer between his shoulder blades that his friends at first thought he was dead. In mortal fear of their lives they all ran off and took refuge in the nearby Bathurst Hotel.

Working methodically, it took the rioters three-quarters of an hour to smash through the great wooden doors with the wedges and iron bars. Every splinter struck off was thrown into the crowd, to the accompaniment of great cheers, and eventually a hole was made big enough for a lad to crawl through. Inside, he drew the iron bolts and the crowd burst in, scattering to the jail blocks. There they released 170 men and women who, intent on hiding their identity as quickly as possible, on that cold and clammy October afternoon, tore off their prison clothes, shoes and all, and ran away almost nude, grabbing at the money offered to them by another very respectable-looking man as they went. Cheering, the mob raised a black flag — it was in fact a very large handkerchief — on the top of the gatehouse, looted everything of value and then wrecked the place. A special target for their wrath was the gallows apparatus which, together with the wagon used for the transportation of felons, was thrown into the New River (the Cut), where the quickly ebbing tide carried them away.

While they were busy about their labours William Herepath, Vice-President of the Bristol Political Union, and some of its members arrived and on announcing who they were were listened to attentively. To no avail, however, for having heard what they had to say the rioters decided to proceed with the destruction of the jail anyway. The man who had dolled out the cash took off his hat, put it on top of his umbrella, waved it and shouted "Now, damn ye, we shall have Reform!! This is what should have been done years go!" To the accompaniment of more cheering the crowd then set fire to the treadmill and Humphries' house and the chapel above it, and were so busy that some of them did not even notice the arrival of twenty soldiers of the 3rd Dragoon Guards. Those who did were not in the least perturbed! Led by a young Cornet called Kelson the men rode up to the gates, waved their hats in acknowledgement of the cheers of the crowd, watched what was going on for a few minutes and then turned "threes about" and trotted back to College Green. In the face of a crowd which by now numbered many thousands there was little else they could do.

In the rain, drunk with wine, success and contempt, the self-appointed leaders of the insurrection sat in the courtyard of the prison, surrounded by flame and smoke, and discussed their next targets. Ships, the Bishop's Palace, banks, The Mansion House and the home in Berkeley Square of a wealthy anti-Reform merchant Tom Daniel were all listed but, no doubt wearied by their exertions, they decided that for the time being it would suffice if the toll booths were flattened. Three were duly set upon and destroyed, at St Philips, Prince's Street Bridge and The Wells.

Up at the Guildhall the Magistrates and Brereton were having a row. Brereton refused to recall the 14th from Keynsham, saying that to do so might imperil their lives. When asked if that was a proper answer for a soldier to give, he replied that soldiers were too valuable for their lives to be sacrificed unnecessarily. When told the city had a right to their protection Brereton responded that while he was quite prepared to risk his own life he was not prepared to jeopardise the lives of men under his command.

Downstairs, something like a hundred citizens who had now gathered in response to the magistrates' call for a public meeting were waiting for a lead, but none was forthcoming. They stood there for hours, willing to act, and saying so, but with no-one to direct them, and complaining about it. The only decision made by the Chief magistrate was that they should all make their way to the Council House, which, he said, would be easier to defend. Thinking that an attack was imminent many of the citizens, some of whom were constables and carried staves, made off home as fast as their legs could carry them.

At about five o'clock William Herepath called at the Council House with a proposal, namely that the swing bridges which linked the area around the New Gaol with the rest of the city should be swung open, marooning the rioters on the island thus created. It was a very good idea (though not perhaps as simple as it sounded since there were not only six bridges but also ten dock gates with a footpath on the top which would also have had to be opened) but it was vetoed by Alderman Hilhouse, who thought the mob would get their revenge by setting fire to his dockyard. . . .

And so the daylight hours of fruitless dithering and pointless discussion passed, a day of constant rain, which increased in force until in late afternoon it was coming down in torrents. At his Recruiting Office on College Green a sodden Lieutenant-Colonel Brereton had taken time off to write to the Military Secretary at the Horse Guards, Major-General Lord Fitzroy Somerset — with whom he had been in communication ever since the decision to send troops to Bristol had been taken and give him his version of events. He said that the mob had "promised earnestly to disperse if the 14th were withdrawn, whom they were otherwise determined to massacre with the aid of the Kingswood men". (He was referring to the miners who hewed coal in the pits about three miles East of the city centre, though whether Lord Fitzroy would understand that is a matter for conjecture.) It was his opinion, Brereton said, that the mood of the rioters had been "strongly excited" by the presence of union men from Birmingham. Only one troop of the 3rd Dragoon Guards remained and they had been on duty for so long that they could not be considered to be in a very efficient state. He was therefore apprehensive that the night would not pass quietly. On that point he was absolutely right.

At dusk the crowd set off for the Gloucestershire County Prison at Lawford's Gate, a mile or so to the East. On the way some youths broke ranks to chase and stone the evening mail coach bound for London. (To one of the passengers the mob seemed to be neither formidable in numbers or organisation; in his opinion fifty London policemen would have been able to deal with it. He did not realise that he was only looking at a fraction of it.) Having established a proven method of sorting out prisons it did not take the mob long to deal with the county jail. Ringing violently at the door-bell they collared the turnkey when he opened it and demanded his keys. Within minutes the twenty-three inmates had been released. Seeing that one, a boy, was in irons the crowd became so incensed that they threw three of Keeper Oatridge's pigs into the flames which they had quickly kindled.

It was all very exhilarating, and breaking up into smaller groups they now began to pick their own targets around the city centre. One band of drunkards demanded ale from the New Inn, another whisky from the Hibernia Tavern near Lawford's Gate — where they beat the landlord up, knocked his sister to the floor and wrecked his house when he argued the toss. Others made their way to the little lock-up in Tailor's Court, off Broad Street, and forced the Sheriff's Sergeant to let the debtors out, while yet another group went back to the Bridewell, stoked up the fires and finished the work of destruction. Lacking an aim, the great majority just roamed around banging at the doors of ale houses and demanding free sustenance; fearful inn keepers complied, and stoked the fires of rebellion.

Major Mackworth reappeared during the evening and found that there were still more than a hundred citizens standing in and around the Council House, engaged in a very lively debate about what should be done. Many were, he said, willing to act, but, as had been the case earlier in the day, protested that they had no-one to direct them. Some said a posse should be formed, but not many were keen to join it. He said he would form one himself, at six o'clock the next morning on College Green, but the response was so lukewarm that, "overcome with disgust" he returned to his friends in Clifton, resolved to do nothing more until the following morning.

Meanwhile the magistrates wrote to the Home Secretary telling him what had been going on. They decided that Brereton should see the letter, since it was highly critical of him, and sent it to him at about 6 pm. It arrived at the same time as the Mayor, who told the colonel that he had heard that the rioters were intent on setting fire to the ships lining the quaysides in the centre of the city. If they did, he said, the results would be absolutely catastrophic; flames would leap from sail to sail and ship to ship, then spread to the warehouses beside them. Whole sections of the city could be engulfed, and there was no way that it could be prevented. Brereton sent Sergeant Dininge — who, according to some of the Aldermen who arrived later was drunk — to find out what was happening, while the letter, in the care of Secretary Burges, was delivered to the Post Office. In due course the scout reported that the crowd were moving towards the cathedral, not the quays.

Fortified, the mob had eagerly rallied round when someone in Queen Square shouted "Now for the Bishop!" and by eight o'clock, chanting "Down with the churches and mend the roads with them!" and "The King and No Bishops!" they had made their way up the little slope to College Green and were battering at the gates of his cloisters. Fortunately for him he had taken the precaution of going to visit a sick daughter who lived at Almondsbury, North-West of the city: it was Jones the Butler who was in charge when the mob arrived, lifted the gates off their hinges and then broke open the door of the Bishop's Palace with a crow bar. Escaping out of a back window Jones made his way around to the front, mingled with the crowd and was there when a small detachment of sixteen dragoons, who had been withdrawn from the square and were now led by Brereton, arrived. Jones asked the colonel if he would order a number of the soldiers to dismount and help him disperse the mob but, not surprisingly, his request was rejected: dismounted, the crowd would have clubbed the dragoons to the ground in no time. However, a few constables and gentlemen, for once firmly acting together, made some arrests and temporarily took the sting out of the situation, tying some of the ringleaders to large casks in a cellar.

The crowd slowly dispersed and re-entering the Palace, Jones found, amongst the litter of smashed glass and furniture, four slashed mattresses into which burning coals had been heaped. He had managed to extinguish the fires and was beginning to tidy the place up when he heard another commotion and, looking out, found to his horror that the soldiers had withdrawn and the crowd had come back to finish its business, fighting with the constables to release the prisoners they had taken on the way. This time there was no stopping them; "within a short space of twenty minutes," as a harassed Reverend Robert Gray was to tell the Home Secretary, his quill pen spattering ink over the paper as he wrote in great haste, "the Palace, with its valuable furniture, books etc. was in flames". He went on to say that "the City of Bristol is at present entirely in the possession of an organised banditti of the vilest and . . . most dastardly description".

Indeed it was; flames leapt into the night sky from the disintegrating roof of the Palace as drunken men and boys, shouting "No bishops, down with the bloody bishops," started a bonfire in the burial ground with priceless old parchments, books and records — including a great Bible bound in red velvet — which they brought from the Chapter-House and fed on to the flames, capering about with great glee as lead poured off the burning roof like water. With the superstitious fear which illiterate people had of the written word, a magic thing which they could not understand, they rushed back and forth tossing ancient and priceless volumes onto the flames. While they did this the wine cellars were plundered and those bottles not consumed quickly went on sale to the watching crowds in the street for a penny or twopence a time. Unable to stand what was going on, some worthy citizens managed to save a few of the scrolls and books from the library, but not before about six thousand of them had been torn up, trampled into the mud or burnt. Despite their threats the mob was somehow persuaded not to set the cathedral itself on fire

— perhaps that deed was too much even for them. (Only the East, choir, part existed. The original nave, built by Black Monks — Augustinians — in the 12th Century had fallen into ruin during the years following Henry VIII's schism with the Roman Catholic church, and was not to be rebuilt until the late-19th Century.)

Back at the Council House a very harassed Pinney was getting no respite. Alderman Camplin arrived to tell him that when the soldiers had been withdrawn from Queen Square to try to quell the new riot at the Bishop's Palace the mob had returned in force to the Mansion House. When he got the usual negative reaction from the magistrates Camplin (who was a brother-in-law of the bishop) went out on to the balcony and asked some people who were in the hall to follow him. About fifty said they would, called on the Mayor to go too and when Pinney appeared at the head of the stairs cheered loudly. (There seems to have been a deal of cheering going on in Bristol on the 30th October 1831, one way and another.) They surged out only to find after a few minutes that he was no longer with them. Some said he had cravenly retreated up the stairs as soon as they started on their way, others that he had only gone back for his hat. Probably that was true, for, accompanied by Ebenezer Ludlow, he followed the group to the Bishop's Palace, arriving at the time when the constables had succeeded in scattering the crowd and making their arrests.

Believing that things were under control, Pinney walked across the Green and went for the second time to see Brereton in the Recruiting Office. Cornet Kelson was there, his very exhausted troop having been withdrawn to stables to feed and rest, and on being asked why he was there and not Captain Warrington, admitted that his commanding officer was nowhere to be found. Pinney himself must have been a very weary man: apart from a few moments of snatched sleep in the Mansion

House the night before he had been on the go without respite or food for a day and a half. He had begun the whole awful sequence of events by meeting Sir Charles Wetherell at the Guildhall, had gone from there to the Mansion House, thence over the rooftops to College Green, back to Queen Square, back to the Guildhall, across to the Council House, from there to the Recruiting Office, back to the Council House, over the well-worn route down Clare Street to the Green again and finally from the cathedral once again to the colonel's office.

The same applied to Brereton, who had hardly been off his feet or horseback for thirty-six hours. He had repeatedly tried to ease the temper of the crowds the evening before and had led the cavalry charge against them, had been in the square first thing to withdraw the picket — and had then gone back again later to try to reason with the mob, had ridden up to the Guildhall to seek agreement to the withdrawal of the 14th, had been summoned there again during the afternoon and had been at the Palace facing the angry crowd again a few minutes before. Now he, Pinney, Ludlow and a few others sat in the bow window and looked out on to the garden of the burning Bishop's Palace, astounded by the flames and appalled by the whole business but hoping against hope that the worst was over.

It was not to be, for within minutes there were cries of "The mob's coming back! Run for it!" Deciding that they would be safer elsewhere they went out into the night and became separated by the crowd, who, fortunately for him, failed to recognise their Mayor, no longer in his finery and getting soaked through because it was unsafe to carry an umbrella; anyone who did was laible to be set upon and knocked down, since it was a badge of privilege. In the darkness, with one of his friends assaulted at his side and his teeth knocked out by a blow, but determined to avoid his own house, only a short distance away, in case he drew the mob there, the terrified Pinney went from pillar to post trying to find a safe anchorage. After trying in vain to get sanctuary in Sheriff Lax's house in Park Street — Lax was very sensibly out of town and had taken the precaution of removing all his valuables out of his house — he made his way to Berkeley Square, at the top of the Park Street hill, from where, looking down on the city, he could see the centre ringed with flame: the jail by the Cut, the jail at the bottom of Pithay, the county jail to the East, the Bishop's Palace, the remains of the toll booths and now, suddenly, the Mansion House.

Seeing the few troops available withdrawn from the square to attend to the disturbances at the Palace the mob had gone back to their first target and had finally put a light to the bonfire which had been prepared twenty-four hours before. With its rooms lined with wooden wainscotting the place went up like a torch and burned with astounding speed, for by the time the troopers had reached the cathedral, only half a mile away, the flames from the mayoral mansion were leaping out of its roof.

Thinking that perhaps the whole thing was a frightful nightmare Mayor Pinney at last found refuge in the house of Mr Daniel Fripp, brother of the Alderman of that name. Bone weary he sank into a chair and had started to write a letter notifying people of his where-abouts when he was interrupted by his host who said that his wife was very apprehensive about the Mayor's pre-sence, in case the mob got to hear of it, and would he please not tell anyone where he was! For all that, word got around, for later that night he was visited by his dutiful secretary Burges, by the Town Clerk and by someone who wanted him to sign a piece of paper sanc-tioning the provision of accommodation for a troop of

Yeomanry who had entered the city. It was the first he had heard about it but in the event his authority was not needed, for the soldiers had already turned about and gone home.

*

Monday, 31st October, 1831

At nine-thirty on the Sunday evening Captain Christopher Codrington had led the fifty men of his troop of the Dodington and Marshfield Yeomanry Cavalry into Bristol. He had received Mayor Pinney's call for help — delivered to him by a Mr James Bush — at 2.30 pm, had bustled about and had managed, by seven o'clock, to muster most of his part-time soldiers and set off. Codrington was twenty-six years old and heir to Sir Christopher Codrington of Dodington Park, a dozen miles away to the North East of the city.

His unit had only been in existence for ten months and it must have been a raw and rather unsure group of uniformed country lads, as likely to slash off their own horse's ears as the heads of the mob if they drew their sabres in anger, who cantered aimlessly through the milling crowds who filled the city centre — and boastfully informed them of the fact that the jails had been emptied of their inhabitants! With blazing buildings around them they trotted about for an hour or so before arriving at the Council House in search of a magistrate. Not finding one, Codrington then went off to the Guildhall, where he again drew a blank, but on going back to the Council House was given a message from the City Chamberlain to report to Colonel Brereton on College Green. Just as his troop had started on their way he was stopped by the Chief Constable of the Castle Precincts Ward, the area just to the North of the Pithay, a jumble of closely-packed houses, shops and alleys, and asked to disperse some drunks who had broken into a gin shop. Codrington replied that he would like to but could not, since he had not heard the Riot Act read.

On arriving at the Recruiting Office Brereton was at first nowhere to be found but soon appeared having, he said, been out "patrolling the streets" on foot. Codrington asked if there was a magistrate available and when Brereton replied that he did not know where to find one told him that his own lieutenant was a Justice of the Peace and could read the Riot Act himself, providing he took his coat off first. Brereton shook his head and said that would not do, and the two of them went off to call on the nearby homes of two magistrates, in the hope that one would come with them. Both had made themselves scarce and were nowhere to be found. Codrington then suggested that Brereton should take the troop to Queen Square, where most of the mob were now concentrating, but the colonel disagreed, and told him to take his men to Fisher's Repository, just around the corner.

When the yeomanry got there they found that the gas pipes had been cut by the crowd who had baited the 14th Light Dragoons earlier in the day and that the place was in darkness. Waiting for lights to be put in the stables Codrington came to the conclusion that anyway the place was too small for his unit and that furthermore he was fed up to the back teeth with the whole business. He had, he decided, had enough. "This is too bad," he said to his sergeant: "I will not be humbugged in this manner any longer," and having made that petulant pronouncement led his men out of the city.

It seems, though, that after taking his bold decision to go off in a huff Codrington had second thoughts, for the troop waited for two hours at Downend, about four miles out "in the hope that they would receive a summons from the authorities". Since the authorities did not know they were there, it is hardly surprising that they received no communication from them. Eventually, after watching the reflection of Bristol's fires in the night sky (which, it was later said, could be seen fifty miles away, and certainly was seen in Frome and Bath, and in Cardiff and Newport across the Severn) they walked their horses homewards, reaching their villages at about five in the morning.

Codrington's story is one of several fiascos in which the military had been involved since the riots began. During the Saturday evening, in Bath, another riot started when Captain Wilkins, in command of the local troop of the North Somerset Yeomanry Cavalry Volunteers, arrived at the White Hart Inn to call his men together to answer the plea from Pinney. He was trapped in the building by a mob of three hundred people who threatened to wreck it if he attempted to take his men to Bristol, and only managed to escape by making a bolt for it, in borrowed civilian clothes, out of a back door. (The rioters then marched off to the Town Hall where they proceeded to smash windows until the local constables restored order at around midnight.) The Bath troop eventually set off to the relief of Bristol on the Monday morning.

On the Sunday morning, while events had been going on apace just across the Bristol Bridge, other soldiers had been available and prepared for action but were never called upon, even though they had been summoned by the magistrates themselves the day before. Captain Shute, commanding the Bedminster troop of the same Yeomanry Cavalry, had taken his men to a riding school near St Mary Redcliffe church and then sent a note to the magistrates, about mid-day, telling them he was there and awaiting their instructions. He waited in vain, for throughout the day none came, and towards evening he and his men decided to go home.

As Sunday passed and his unit was sent hither and yon for no good reason, and succeeded only in becoming more and more tired and dispirited, Captain Warrington of the 3rd Dragoons was heard to observe that in his opinion "there was a great screw loose somewhere". That evening, feeling unwell and ill at ease, he left his unit and went, on foot in the pouring rain, up to Clifton, to the home of Major-General Pearson, to ask his advice on whether it was absolutely essential to have a magistrate present when troops went into action in aid of the civil power. Warrington was no stranger to this situation, having himself been involved in the agricultural riots the year before, but there had always been a magistrate present on those occsions and now, though it was obvious that strong measures were necessary, none were being taken. Much perplexed by what was going on he trudged up the hill to seek guidance but whether he got any seems unlikely, for the General sent him packing from Prospect Cottage and within four minutes of entering it he was on his way down the hill again. . . .

He had been billeted in Reeve's Hotel on the Green. Reaching it at about nine pm, one of the women there told him he looked very unwell and should go to bed, which he did. Later, it was alleged, when one of his noncommissioned officers came to tell him that his troop had been called out on duty Warrington told him to push off, for he was not interested. . . . However, he was eventually prevailed upon to rouse himself since the mob decided to attack the very place in which he rested! The ten young hooligans who were stoning the hostelry were quickly dispersed. Later when Warrington, in the Horse Bazaar with his unit, was asked by a Mr Kington to go to Queen Square, where things were totally out of control, he demurred, saying he would be only too pleased to oblige but could not move without directions from Colonel Brereton, whose whereabouts he did not know.

*

At two o'clock on that Sunday night Pinney was penning a letter to his wife at the Clifton Hotel, in the Mall. "My dearest love," he wrote, "Keep as calm as possible. . and as quiet as possible. . . . I will not place myself in danger. . . . Pray for Divine aid to help and preserve us in this trying occasion." He signed it "Yours ever afffectionately, Charles." Later in the day Mrs Pinney and her mother were asked to leave the hotel by the proprietor because the other guests were nervous about having them there in case the mob should hear of it and attack the hotel.

The owner of the hotel need not have worried about the mob for they had no need to go up the hill when all they could ask for was close at hand. While the Major, the magistrates, the military and the population in general were being either indecisive, inept, ineffective or indifferent the mob, the few who had become the many, abetted by a multitude, now went, without any hindrance at all, about the serious business of subjecting a great area of the city to plunder and arson. First of all, just before the picket of dragoons were withdrawn to the Bishop's Palace, a small group crept into the back of the sixty-year-old Mansion House and raided the cellars, passing out to their waiting comrades the remains of the mayoral wine stock. Then others followed them in and made their way upstairs to steal whatever they could lay their hands on, throwing furniture and bedding out of the windows to the hooting and whistling crowd below. Some went into the pantries and carted off the spoils: kegs of flour and sugar, jars of preserved fruits and pickles, game birds and joints of meat. One young boy was seen to take away a lump of beef and jam it high in the branches of a tree for safe keeping while he went back for more; a man staggered off with a side of bacon, and another with a leg of mutton under each arm.

The few dragoons, meanwhile, remained sitting astride their droop-necked horses and watched what was happening with resignation. They were so few in number that there was no possibility of them stopping the huge crowd from doing what they wanted and it must have been with something like relief that they received the news that they were needed elsewhere. The effect of their departure was, however, electric, since it signalled the withdrawal of the very last token of control. In a flash word went around and horse-drawn carts and hand barrows were soon being trundled into the square. Before long many of the city treasures had vanished into the nether regions. Even a grand piano was lugged down the stairs by six Irishmen and sold to a gentleman in Back Street for two guineas — who subsequently returned it to the Corporation. And had it not been for the presence of mind of three people many more valuable things would have vanished too.

During one of the periodic lulls the day before Isambard Kingdom Brunel, who acted as a special constable when not engaged on planning the Great Western Railway, had saved most of the paintings, including a Van Dyke and Lawrence, by cutting them out of the frames and walking off with the canvases rolled up in a small carpet. A few hours later a Mr Smith rescued the beautiful, gold-encrusted Great (or Lent) Sword, which the

City Swordbearer had very carelessly left behind when he made a hurried exit; at the same time a Mr Burroughs managed to pack silver and money into servant's trunks and get them through the throng. But by far the greater part of the contents were pillaged, and then the place was put to the torch. This time, instead of sending people rushing around looking for a light, a youth climbed a nearby gas lamp, lit a candle at the flame there then nursed it back to the turpentine! In less than an hour, in a great roar of flame and sparks, the building collapsed, a sight which finally dispelled any remaining restraint there had been in the milling crowds and triggered off hours of frenetic mania.

The Custom House was the next to be set upon, emptied of valuables and then put to the torch. A large party of people sitting stuffing themselves with food in the housekeeper's room next to the second-floor kitchen were burnt to death when flames lit by their compatriots, unaware that they were there, trapped them. Some fried, three leapt off the roof to escape but died on the flagstones below; just before he expired, one of them said "Oh, that I had taken my wife's advice and never come to Bristol!" Just as the roof fell in a man toppled out of the end window and crashed to the ground, dreadfully burnt, while a group who had mistakenly sheltered under the portico were wrapped in molten metal when its lead covering heated, boiled, glowed and then engulfed them.

Elsewhere, ignoring these appalling scenes, enterprising citizens set up shop, selling everything imaginable to whoever would buy: a silver tea-pot for a shilling, a mahogany chair for half-a-crown. Some did buy, for a penny or two, things worth pounds, but many did not, for why buy when you could help yourself? As the hours passed many of the houses in the square were stripped of their contents, which were then lugged away. And while all this was happening a great throng of "respectable" Bristolians stood in the background sniggering or tut-tutting but doing nothing to stop the pillage. At the height of the disturbance about twenty-thousand people were involved in or watching the pandemonium.

It was not long before the mob came to the conclusion that official property was not yielding enough and that the adjoining houses of the well-to-do would be a better source of the world's riches. They did not have it all their own way and here and there were repulsed, if only temporarily, but a few brave souls could not deter the mass who were surging around demanding blood, booty and fire. Soon people were sitting in the square on stolen chairs, swilling stolen wine and eating stolen food off stolen tables; shouting and blaspheming while walls, roofs, beams and rafters crashed down all around them. When wine ran short it was but a short run to get more from the nearest broached cellar.

Individuals, of course, spent their energy, filled themselves or their pockets and then collapsed unconscious or staggered home with their booty but the mob now had a life of its own and when some fell out others took their place. At one point a crowd of three hundred men, women and children, already half drunk from the wine and beer stolen from the houses they had raided, spilled up the road to the Horse Fair and demanded that the landlord of the White Horse Inn should serve them with ale, threatening to burn the place around his ears if he was not quick about it: they gave him three minutes to dress himself and do as he was told and then drank his stock dry. At the Bank Tavern four men drank three pints of raw spirits in five minutes, shouting "Damn you, give us more gin!" Old scores were paid off too: while bands of thieves prowled the city some of the prisoners freed from the jails returned to claim retribution from those who had consigned them to jail.

Back in the square it was the turn of the Excise Office, and after it the Custom's Bonding Warehouse. When the mob assaulted Captain Claxton's house his negro servant, chosen to stay and work in Bristol rather than go to the West Indies on sale, repayed his employer by throwing a shrieking woman out of a first-floor window when she attempted to steal some of his master's property. (She lay without moving for hours but no-one could say, later, if she had lived or died.) Another owner of a house, given twenty minutes to get out before the mob surged in, was so angry at seeing some of his belongings vandalised that he too threw the offender out of a window. (A newspaper reporter subsequently regretted that "the circumstances did not occur at a sufficient elevation to ensure the destruction of the villain".) In yet another house a servant woman was knocked unconscious when she tried to reason with the intruders. But these were isolated incidents in a saga of events which saw the rioters looting and burning their way unhindered through the houses on the North and West sides of the square and into adjoining streets. A private collection of seventeen hundred books was destroyed in a bonfire danced around by crazy people. As the riot spread business premises too were engulfed: huge quantities of Fry's cocoa went up in smoke as did many barrels of rum in Johnson's warehouse. They burst, and sent a river of flame down the street. Women running through it to safety had their smouldering clothes smothered by seamen who happened to be there.

At last two of the owners of Queen Square property decided that enough was enough: Samuel Goldney and Wintour Harris Junior found their way to Berkeley Square and asked Daniel Fripp if he knew where a magistrate was to be found. When he said that the Chief Magistrate was within they demanded to see the Mayor.

Under their direction, at three o'clock on the Monday morning, Charles Pinney wrote to "Colonel Brereton or the Commanding Officer of His Majesty's Troops" directing whoever it was to take the most vigorous, effective and decisive means in his power to quell the riot and prevent further destruction of property.

Brereton was in fact in bed, in 2, Unity Street, two hundred yards from the Recruiting Office, in the lodgings of his Adjutant, Lieutenant Francis, which he had intended to make his domestic base since the troubles began on the Saturday morning but which he had not, so far, had time to enter. He had come to the conclusion that "it was impossible, in the absence of any magistrate, or indeed the smallest appearance of a civil force, to be of any service with the then few exhausted troops" he had, and that since that was the situation there was no point in hanging around waiting for people who were themselves safely tucked up out of harm's way in places unknown. However, like Pinney, he was not to get any sleep for a second night running.

Having secured the Mayor's authorisation Goldney and Harris trudged off to Leigh's Horse Bazaar to find Captain Warrington. He, given the magisterial authority he had been seeking for so long, said that while he would like to co-operate he could do nothing without Colonel Brereton's agreement, adding that he did not expect to see him before six am and repeating that in his view there was a great screw loose somewhere. Furious, Goldney and Harris retreated. An hour later Warrington told Alderman Camplin that he thought his troops were too few in number to have a decisive effect on the rioters. When told that Camplin was a magistrate and would accompany the troops Warrington agreed to send some to Queen Square, but when told that he should go himself, backed off, saying that he would do nothing without the colonel's authorisation. At last he gave in and went with Camplin to wake Brereton, but when they got to number 2, Unity Street two women leaned out of an upstairs bedroom window and denied that he was there!

He was, though, and was soon leading twenty-one dragoons into Queen Square (leaving Warrington in charge of a reserve of eleven men). In a matter of a few hours strong but belated disciplinary action had restored order and the city was left smoking, shattered and licking its wounds.

*

Aftermath

Early on the morning of Monday the 31st October
1831 Tom Brereton, at the head of the small detachment
of 3rd Dragoons, charged down Prince Street, across
Queen Square (despite the fact that about two thousand
people were in it) and ended up outside Number 42, the
home of Captain Claxton, which was then being plundered by the mob. Dismounting, some of the troopers
went to the assistance of Robert Hopton, his negro
servant — he who had thrown a woman on to the paving
stones below a front window — managed to douse the
fires that had been lit and chased the raiders out. Emerg-
ing, a few were immediately cut down by the sabres of
the waiting soldiers, who had had more than enough.
Brereton, true to form, ordered them to desist from
violence but just at that moment Major Mackworth
reappeared. Shouting "Colonel, we must instantly
charge!" he did not wait for his superior officer to
answer but called out "Charge, men, and charge home!"
which the soldiers duly did, "with the utmost alacrity"
and led by Brereton, brandishing his sword!

Many people were cut down or ridden over, and quite a few were driven into burning buildings, out of which they did not emerge. After sabreing all they could stretch out to in the square the soldiers reformed and charged down Prince Street, then came about, reformed again and charged once more through the square. It was not a rout: the rioters were game to the last and met the cavalry with volleys of stones and a shot or two from firearms (one dragoon was wounded in the arm) but the "miserable mob", though so many in number, were no match for the few soldiers. Panting, the 3rd Dragoon Guards at last drew reign and breath and looked around at the rapidly emptying scene of ruin. Dozens of buildings were on fire, many of which had collapsed into great heaps of rubble. The dead lay where they had fallen amidst littered furniture and carpets, indistinguishable from the drunks, while many wounded, moaning men were sprawled on the trampled muddy grass or were being dragged out of sight by women and children.

Mackworth obtained Brereton's permission to recall the 14th from Keysham and rode off to get them, begging the colonel "to keep the square with the 3rd as long as it was in his power," which, assisted by Captain Warrington and the small reserve who had joined him, he contrived to do with no great difficulty. As the weary dragoons patrolled about, from time to time beating off the more persistent rioters who thought their day had not yet ended, a new character made his appearance at the Council House, having arrived in haste by post-chaise from Gloucester in advance of another troop of his regiment, the 14th Light Dragoons. Major William Beckwith, 35 years of age, was an experienced and self-confident soldier who, in his 'teens, had seen service in the Peninisular War and fought at the battle of Waterloo.

Reporting to Mayor Pinney Beckwith found him and his fellow magistrates "stupified with terror", and when he asked that some of the aldermen accompany him to Queen Square was assured by them that they would be only too pleased to but they could not ride — an extraordinary admission by gentlemen who, in those days, learnt that accomplishment at a very early age. However, he managed to prise from them a written authority for the restoration of peace and with that indispensable document in his pocket went off to the scene of action. Perhaps he too remembered that after the militia had been called out to quell a riot in 1793 there had been an official enquiry into their conduct.

On arriving in the square Brereton told him that the 14th were on their way back from Keynsham, and then said he was going back to the Green and would be obliged if Beckwith would "wait upon him at Number 9 in an hour". When Beckwith complied with this order the colonel was not there, but was eventually run to earth at 2, Unity Street, where he was putting on fresh linen. Brereton seemed more than ever like a man in a dream, totally remote from the realities of the appalling situation which had inexorably evolved during the past two days. He said the magistrates were useless, that they had refused to give him written orders but that even if they had he had too few troops available to deal with the situation.

Beckwith was to give him the lie on that point, for when the troop returned from Keynsham, in company with a few part-time soldiers of the Bedminster Yeomanry Cavalry who had joined them en route, he took command and proceeded to sort out the mob. Mounting a borrowed horse he took his men across the Green to the Bishop's Palace, scattered scavengers picking for loot amongst the ruins, and then, at about 10 am, cantered down to the square. There and in the vicinity, for two whole hours, the 3rd and 14th dragoons vented their pent-up frustration and wrath with no holds barred. "In the most spirited manner" they charged repeatedly across the square, scattering the crowd in all directions, and then pursued running, screaming people down the side streets, riding along the pavements cutting and swiping at everyone in their way, even those who cowered in corners. Men and women, and children too, fled in terror before the slashing blades. For his pains one man who attempted to grab the bridle of one of the dragoon's horses had his head completely severed from his shoulders and at the end of Castle Street a very powerful man, who had been urging the crowd to hold their ground, had his head severed too by the back-handed slash from a dragoon. Another had his nose and upper lip cut off. One of the soldiers broke two sabres. Another used his scabbard as a blade when his was broken. Regrettably, in the midst of all this melee a twelve-year-old boy, Tom Morris, was killed by a shot fired by a half-pay Captain by the name of Lewis who was acting as a constable. Lewis had to be rescued from an infuriated mob by his fellow constables, who made more arrests. In all, something like a hundred people were hauled off to improvised lock-ups, but they were just a tiny fraction of the great horde who had taken part in or abetted the rioting.

While Major Beckwith was dealing out vengeance the other major started to organise army and navy pensioners into groups who quickly established themselves in control of the city. As cavalry reinforcements began to arrive from Tetbury, Wells and Devizes Major Mackworth positioned them on the main roads, with orders to disperse any persons illegally assembling and seal off the city. Word had reached the country districts and groups of ten or twenty people, many of them armed with bludgeons, were hurrying to the source of plunder. As they passed turnpikes and churches they shook their fists and hurled abuse, threatening to level them all on their return journey. (Brereton, it seems, had had as much as he could take — he must have been physically exhausted, after all, apart from being in a state of mental confusion — and played no part in restoring order.)

By mid-day, when all danger had passed, five thousand or so citizens rallied to the defence of their city and enrolled as special constables, wearing a strip of white linen around their right arms to identify them from ordinary people. Pinney too, in a surge of confidence, became decisive and issued notices to the effect that the POSSE COMITATUS (a body of citizens given legal powers to maintain law and order) had been called out, and telling people "not engaged in official duties as Constables to keep within their respective Dwellings as they will otherwise be exposed to the most imminent Peril". In a second notice he asked everyone to place Lights in the Windows; it was feared that the mob were going to cut off the gas supply, plunge the city into darkness and start their work of destruction all over again. But he need not have worried: the people had had their fling and were now in their hovels nursing sabre cuts or snoring in an exhausted stupor.

Throughout the Monday shops remained shut as the posse was organised and deployed. The contents of houses which had been pillaged littered the square as special constables climbed over the still-smoking rubble searching for bodies. Dozens of charred remains were found and in the wreck of the Mansion House a blackened man with an arm apparently burned off at the shoulder suddenly threw off charred timbers, got up, shook his head and staggered off! As the hours passed smouldering buildings burst into flame without warning while burning brandy in a cellar in King Street made part of the pavement erupt. Rumours raced around that the mob were at their evil work again but it was not so: the short, sharp shock of the sabres had done their work and the guilty ones sobered up to the realisation that the mighty arm of English law was about to crack down on them. Fearing the repercussions that were sure to descend on them too, Pinney and the magistrates decided to send letters to the Home Secretary and to the Commander-in-Chief of the Army, excusing their conduct and blaming Brereton for what had happened. Having agreed upon that course of action they went off home, Pinney for the first time in four days.

That day Captain Codrington had written to no less a person than Lord Melbourne to tell him that "having patrolled the city for two hours without being able to find a magistrate, hearing that they had left town after withdrawing His Majesty's troops and the police; finding himself unsupported, and the city in the uncontrolled power of the mob, he had had no alternative but to withdraw his men". Soon after finishing this letter he received one from the Mayor of Bristol, in which Pinney said the magistrates deeply regretted their absence from the Council House when Codrington arrived — which, he said, had been due to them having had to lead a body of citizens to a distant part of the city in performance of an arduous duty. (He was referring to the fact that he and one or two others had been watching the Bishop's Palace burn when the yeomanry arrived.) He was sorry this had deprived them of the pleasure of seeing him, but thanked him for his prompt response to their call for help. No disrespect was intended, Pinney assured the young aristocrat; on the contrary, the magistrates duly appreciated his kind intentions and begged him, should he decide to come to the city again, to send a sergeant on ahead in order that proper arrangements could be made for the troop's reception. . . .

As dusk came infantry under the command of Lieutenant-Colonel Love arrived from Cardiff and marched down an apparently deserted Park Street.. However, when Love ordered the battalion drums to be beaten window sashes were flung up, doors were opened and the street quickly filled with people applauding the "brave fellows" who had come "to deliver them from pillage and death". In the city, churches were illuminated and used as temporary accommodation for off-duty troops and constables, and in the windows of houses candles burned through the night. By Tuesday morning things were nearly back to normal and by Wednesday irate merchants, bankers and traders of the city had recovered enough to sit down together and pen yet another letter to Lord Melbourne, deploring the disgraceful proceedings that had recently occurred in the city and earnestly requesting his Lordship to set in train a formal investigation of what had happened, that being the only way in which confidence could be restored.

The government were now in no doubt about the feelings of Bristolians about Reform and sent despatches to garrisons in Woolwich, Portsmouth, Pembroke, Plymouth, Dublin, Cork and Waterford telling them to be prepared to send soldiers to Bristol, while the Admiralty sent frigates into the Bristol Channel. It was all a far cry from the grudging allocation of three troops of cavalry only two weeks earlier.

As the days passed the city made an inventory of its losses: the Mansion House, the Custom House, the Excise Office, three prisons, two chapels, three governor's houses, the Bishop's Palace, the cathedral library, four toll booths, public buildings in Broad Street and more than fifty houses and warehouses between Welsh Back and St Mary Recliffe. Of the houses, nine belonged to merchants, eight were boarding houses, four were owned by accountants, one by a solicitor, one by an architect and one by a bookie. One was a ladies' Boarding School, another was a Dancing Academy and the rest were private dwellings. Though at first the cost of the damage was estimated to be little short of half a million sterling, a more conservative assessment later put the value of destroyed goods at less than £200,000. Even so, no place in England had ever suffered such destruction — and at the hands of its own citizens. While armed soldiers stood on guard in the infirmary at the bedsides of suspected rioters the tidying up of the area around Queen Square was put in hand amidst the stench of putrefying corpses.

According to Major Mackworth, about a hundred and twenty of the rioters were killed and at least another hundred were wounded, including some miners from Kingswood who were chased up the Gloucester Road. (The colliers had a record of violence and some, no doubt, took part in the riot but there is no evidence that they were the ringleaders.) As Beckwith was to write: "A great number of civilian lives were lost. Everything was done at a gallop and with the sword and, in consequence, for one that was killed a hundred were wounded." Most of their opponents, he was sure, did not belong to Bristol, as was shown "by the number of broken heads that were (later) to be seen on every road leading from the town". When someone asked the driver of the Mail Coach what state Bristol had been in when he left replied that "it was most dreadful beyond description; he had counted four and twenty bodies beside the road". But while many of the casualties were members of the mob many of them were not. As a riled citizen was to put it "resistance having ceased, the magistrates became a right valiant lot and respectable citizens were given up to the unbridled passions of the 14th".

The official list put the number of dead at 12 (3 from sword cuts, 2 shot, 6 burned to death and 2 from excessive consumption of alcohol) and the wounded at 96 (10 shot, 49 cut and the rest from "other causes") but according to a subsequent report in The Dublin Evening Post the authorities in Bristol had admitted that 348 people died or were maimed but that those taken off to private houses might well have brought the number to four or five hundred. Furthermore, things being what they were in those days, the great majority of the wounded would have died from blood poisoning or gangrene. Nobody knows how many succumbed for no records were kept, and many of the wounded, guilty and innocent alike, perished for fear of retribution should they try to get help from doctors or the infirmary. For example, in Marsh Street an Irishman was found sitting beside a fire in an upper room severely wounded by a sabre cut which had taken the flesh from his shoulder down to his elbow but when constables offered to take him to have his wound dressed he refused. (Under a rug on a bed in the corner of the room lay the body of the husband of the woman who was in the room, his head cleaved open by a sabre.) In addition, an unknown number perished in the flames of buildings which they or their fellow rioters put to the torch. It was all rather difficult to believe in an age which prided itself on being very enlightened and God-fearing.

On the 1st of November the Deputy Quartermaster General, Major-General Sir Richard Jackson, arrived at the double from London to take command of the troops in and being sent to Bristol, which included guns and 1,5000 rounds of ammunition. On the 2nd the King issued a Royal Proclamation condemning the outrages recently committed in Derby, Nottingham and the city of Bristol, commanding municipal and judicial bodies to repress all tumults and breaches of the peace and his liege subjects to do their bounden duty and enforce the law. On the 3rd the letters written for the mayor by Secretary Burges were finally despatched.

The same day Brereton wrote to Lord Fitzroy Somerset explaining that he had been caught between an infuriated mob and a pusillanimous magistracy. Soldiers and horses had been exhausted, he said, and had he fired on the mob they would have destroyed the troops while they were at rest. Furthermore, when he sent the 14th out of the city, with the concurrence of the mayor, he had been expecting more soldiers to arrive to take their place. He assured his Lordship that he had done his very best throughout the whole "calamitous business." (Unfortunately for Brereton his command of English was not as succinct as this account would suggest and he therefore did not make the most of his case.)

On the 4th, Colonel Love's four companies of infantry from the 11th of Foot were replaced by six companies of the 52nd, only just returned from a tour of duty in America and sent directly from Portsmouth, while in London the Home Secretary replied to the mayor of Bristol's letter by return of post, saying that he greatly lamented the riots and would like to know why the jails, which he presumed were strong buildings, had not been properly defended. In near panic the search started for scapegoats and Pinney released to local newspapers copies of his letters to Lord Melbourne and Lord Hill.

On the 15th General Jackson paraded all his troops, including the guns of the Royal Horse Artillery, in Queen Square and read a message from the Commander-in-Chief in which he praised all the officers and soldiers involved during the riots except Brereton and Warrington. On the 17th a Military Court of Enquiry, consisting of Major-General Sir James Dalbiac and four other officers, convened in the Merchant's Hall, King Street, to ascertain whether there were grounds to pros-

Cavalry cutting down rioters.
(Courtesy of the City of Bristol Museum & Art Gallery).

CHRISTOPHER DAVIS.

RICHARD VINES.

Five convicted men: Christopher Davis, Thomas Gregory,
William Clarke, Joseph Kayes, Richard Vines.
(Courtesy of Bristol Record Office).

JOSEPH KAYES.

THOMAS GREGORY.

WILLIAM CLARKE.

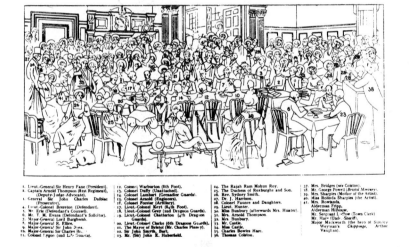

1. Lieut.-General Sir Henry Fane (President).
2. Captain Arnold Thompson (81st Regiment), (Deputy-Judge Advocate).
3. General Sir John Charles Dalbiac (Prosecutor).
4. Lieut.-Colonel Brereton (Defendant).
5. Mr. Erle (Defendant's Counsel).
6. Mr. T. M. Evans (Defendant's Solicitor).
7. Major-General Lord Burghersh.
8. Major-General R. Ellice.
9. Major-General Sir John Buss.
10. Major-General Sir Charles Br...
11. Colonel Lygon (2nd Life Guards).

12. Colonel Warburton (8th Foot).
13. Colonel Duffy (Unattached).
14. Colonel Lambert (Grenadier Guards).
15. Colonel Arnold (Engineers).
16. Colonel Forster (Artillery).
17. Lieut.-Colonel Kerr (84th Foot).
18. Lieut.-Colonel Grey (2nd Dragoon Guards).
19. Lieut.-Colonel Chatterton (4th Dragoon Guards).
20. Lieut.-Colonel Clarke (6th Dragoon Guards).
21. The Mayor of Bristol (Mr. Charles Pinney).
22. Sir John Smyth, Bart.
23. Mr. (Sir) John K. Haberfield.

24. The Rajah Ram Mohun Roy.
25. The Duchess of Roxburghe and Son.
26. Rev. Sydney Smith.
27. Dr. J. Harrison.
28. Colonel Faunce and Daughters.
29. Lieut. Hunter.
30. Miss Bunbury (afterwards Mrs. Hunter).
31. Mrs. Arnold Thompson.
32. Mrs. Bunbury.
33. Mr. Castle.
34. Miss Castle.
35. Charles Bowles Hare.
36. Thomas Colston.

37. Mrs. Bridges (née Colston).
38. Mr. George Powell (Bristol Mercury).
39. Mrs. Sharples (Mother of the Artist).
40. Miss Rolinda Sharples (the Artist).
41. Mrs. Rowlands.
Alderman Fripp.
Alderman Hilhouse.
Mr. Sergeant Ludlow (Town Clerk).
Mr. Hare (Under-Sheriff).
Major Mackworth (the hero of Stanley Weymann's *Chippinge*, Arthur Vaughan).

The Trial of Colonel Brereton. (& Keyplan).
Painting. Rolinda Sharples.
(Courtesy of the City of Bristol Museum & Art Gallery).

'Last Sorrowful Lamentation'.
(Courtesy of the City of Bristol Museum & Art Gallery).

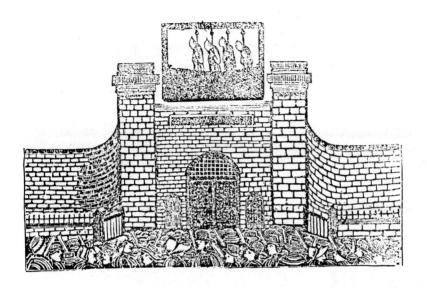

'Trial and Execution of Clarke, Davis, Gregory and Kayes'.
(Courtesy of Bristol Record Office).

View of the City of Bristol. S. Jackson, c. 1831.

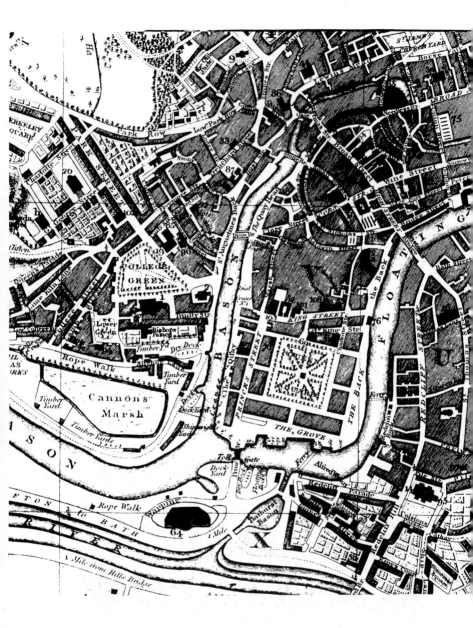

Contemporary Map & Street Plan of Bristol.

ecute Lieutenant Colonel Brereton for failing in his duty. Though the enquiry lasted a week Brereton was away for three days due to indisposition, during which time an officer friend produced on his behalf a twenty-three page explanation by Brereton of what had happened. In it he said that while he had had hardly any rest or food throughout the whole time of the rioting the magistrates who now sought to blame him for what had happened never failed to retire at the appropriate time to a comfortable home, and many of them to their country houses. During his twenty three years service, he said, he had never more strenuously exerted himself for the public good than during the three days "of the late dreadful events in the city."

Despite his defence the court concluded, in the light of evidence given by the mayor, two aldermen, and the Town Clerk, amongst others, that while the magistrates were not blameless in the matter Brereton had been at fault in not displaying "that degree of judgement, activity and firmness generally required of him". Their report, and one on the conduct of Captain Warrington, was sent to Whitehall. One week later, Brereton and Warrington were told that they were to be tried by Court Martial, and that they were to consider themselves under arrest.

In London a special commission was appointed to try the prisoners who were being held for having taken part in the riots while on the 16th November, Melbourne wrote to the merchants of Bristol agreeing that it seemed as if a full investigation of the conduct of the civil and military authorities was required. The scene was set for the Court Martial of two officers, the trial of nearly a hundred prisoners and an investigation into the conduct of the mayor and the magistrates.

*

The Trials

In Bristol the people waited expectantly for the law to take its course — there would be public hangings, that was for sure, something to look forward to in the dull winter days after Christmas — while in London Recorder Wetherell told Parliament that he was most upset that he and the Mayor and Corporation of the city were to be excluded from the Special Commission set up to try the rioters. In his opinion the Bristol Political Union's condemnation of him and the city's authorities had been instrumental in causing the Government to reach that decision, but for the Government Mr George Lamb replied that he was sure that Sir Charles, with his high sense of honour, would wish the inquiry to be totally impartial. . ..

The Union had not been alone in criticising the handling of the affair, though some people said that Mayor Pinney was a dupe, voted into his position as the first citizen of the city by the Tories in anticipation of trouble which could then be blamed on a Whig mayor. Some even went so far as to say that the Tory magistrates, far from being anxious to avoid trouble, actually courted it because they hoped that bad behaviour by the Reformers would go against their cause; as things turned out, they had miscalculated, and the whole thing had got completely out of hand. The newspapers too had a field day and supported their editorial point of view to the full, with accusation and counter-accusation: the Mercury blamed the magistrates for provoking the whole thing by hiring constables (at three shillings and sixpence a day, if you please, a scandalous waste of public money) while "Felix Farley" said the Reformers were entirely to blame. Captain Codrington wrote to the editor of the Bristol Mirror arrogantly justifying his actions, having seen that Mr Pinney, feathered hat in hand, had already tried to justify his by releasing to the Press copies of his letters to Lords Hill and Melbourne. Various Aldermen also had their printed say, all of which was read by just a few literate people in pubs, and then inwardly digested and solemnly pronounced upon by many others. One way and another there was a deal of discussion and bickering in Bristol in the last two months of 1831, most of it bitterly critical of the Corporation, but as is the way in human affairs there was also much pleasure to be had from the excitement generated by the riots and their aftermath.

The use of fireworks had been banned on Guy Fawkes Day, there having been enough of that sort of thing to last a long time, but as compensation there were daily revelations which made interesting gossip. Sometimes the arm of the law was too short or too ponderous and constables arrived to find bonfires burning or incriminating evidence floating off down the Cut or one of the rivers, but quite often they found what they were looking for: a well was stuffed with furniture, two twin-team wagon-loads of stolen goods were retrieved from a house in Host Street, a steep hill just behind what is now the Colston Hall, and Marsh Street, St James's Back and the Dings, dingy parts of the city, were full of plunder. The parish constables who were given authority to scour the poorest places found every conceivable article of loot stashed away in roof spaces, under floorboards, up chimneys, or buried in back gardens under newly-dug earth; so much that the Exchange was designated as the special repository for the sorting of retrieved goods, which were then taken to churches for safe keeping until they could be restored to their owners. Intoxicated people were found lying on reeking cots under which were unopened bottles of wine; silver cutlery was boiling in a saucepan of soup; illiterate people had suddenly learned to read the books on theology which lay incongruously on their scruffy tables; tramps clothed in rags had pockets full of golden sovereigns; men who had never had a bean to spare for years were unaccountably standing drinks in ale houses. . . .

But while peace returned to the city its Aldermen did not sleep well at night, being much concerned that the Commission would be the cause of further disturbances. To be on the safe side they decided to call out a hundred Army pensioners and arm half of them with muskets. Also living in the city, their names listed with quill pen on parchment in the Council House, were around seventeen hundred citizens who were alleged to be prepared to assist in the maintenance of law and order when the occasion demanded, but most of these worthies had been conspicuous by their absence before and throughout the riots and were scarcely more willing to serve now: by the end of November only six hundred and eighty two of them had been persuaded to come forward though Pinney, on the 1st of January 1832, the day before the Commission started its proceedings, wrote to inform Lord Melbourne that fourteen hundred special constables had been enrolled. The Home Secretary had already been told by Major-General Jackson that Bristol's constables were an "ill-composed and most inefficient" lot and had decided that they should be under the command of a very experienced Metropolitan Police Superintendent by the name of Dowling.

The great fear of the authorities was that because the jails had largely been destroyed the mob would endeavour to free the prisoners before they came to trial. Some urgent work had been done to make the battered New Gaol secure but things were not as they should have been and therefore General Jackson disposed his troops around the city centre while the large body of constables were used to provide a round-the-clock watch on the prisoners. Special arrangements were also made for the safety of the Judges when they arrived and during their stay in the city, but in the event when, on Monday the 2nd of January 1832, the Chief Justice of the Common Pleas, Sir Nicolas Tindal, accompanied by Mr Justice Taunton and Mr Justice Bosanquet, made their heavily guarded ceremonial entry from Totterdown only a handful of citizens bothered to turn out to watch them; it was an exceptionally cold day and, besides, few felt inclined to risk having their skull cracked by a cudgel swung by a twitchy constable.

After changing into their robes of office at number 6, Park Street, which had been prepared for use as their lodgings during the course of the trials, the Judges went to the cathedral for Divine Service then made their way to the Guildhall, where a special gallery had been constructed, the better to allow more citizens to witness the proceedings; and where, at two o'clock, they sat in solemn judgement on the first case: five youths and one man were charged with riotous assembly, pulling down the New Gaol and setting fire to Governor Humphries' house. In all, the trials lasted until the 14th of January.

Only one of those found guilty of taking part in the riots was unemployed; most of them were skilled or semi-skilled workmen and artisans — carpenters, bakers, stonemasons. Six owned property but the rest lived in cheap lodging houses in the crowded parts of the city. The rage of rebellion had gripped men who must have been at the limits of their patience with the system under which they lived.

Ten men who had been held prisoner under suspicion of participating in the riots were not proceeded against. Of the 102 people taken before the judges 81 were convicted and 21 acquitted. 31 were sentenced to death but only 4 were actually hung. Sentence of Death was pronounced on 23 men for destroying property, including:

James Coleman, for robbery,

Henry Crinks, Joseph Thomas and David James, for stealing spirits,

James Price and James Dyer, for stealing four gallons of beer, and

James Walker, for obtaining, by force, one quart of beer.

Of the 27 reprieved, 20 were transported for life and 7 were given hard labour. Of the other 50 men and women convicted, 7 were transported and 43 were imprisoned with hard labour. (James Street was transported for seven years for stealing five gallons of wine which belonged to Miss Davey; Joseph Keates also got seven years in the Antipodes for stealing a violin but Sarah Cox, who stood in the dock with her baby in her arms, was found not guilty.) The heaviest jail sentence, for manslaughter, was two years (given to 9 men, including one by the name of Edward Macdonald) and the lightest one month. Catherine Hogan got twelve months for stealing a silk dress; Benjamin Donne was done for taking a brass weight belonging to the King; Tom Brimnell got six months hard labour for stealing a bible and a boy by the name of Daniel Doyle got that, and a whipping too, for stealing a watch.

All in all, considering the havoc wreaked, the destruction, vandalism and theft, the guilty ones got away very lightly, and most of them Scot free. Even those who were convicted were not viciously sentenced, leading one to think that perhaps the judges had a sneaking feeling that the true culprits had never been caught. The four who died were fools rather than knaves, the real villains were never prised out of their hovels and as for the thousands of women who had egged on their men and themselves perpetrated a thousand outrages, not one was put on trial for those offences, but only for petty theft.

One of the most enterprising of the looters was a "respectable looking" Mr James Ives, who stole a large, silver, Elizabethan salver from the Mansion House and then cut it into 167 pieces before trying to sell it. The jeweller to whom he took it was suspicious, and Mr Ives got fourteen years in Australia during which to regret having been caught. (The salver was riveted together and plated with gold and is now one of the city's finest treasures. Only one tiny triangular piece was lost, but another was cleverly substituted, and it is now very difficult to see that anything is missing.)

After the excitement of the judicial hearings, which lasted for two weeks and were avidly followed in the packed public gallery and in newspaper reports, the fact that the men under sentence of death were clearly not vicious criminals dawned upon Bristolians, leaving them with a nasty feeling of guilt which they tried to assuage by speedily petitioning for the punishments to be commuted. More than ten-thousand signatures were on the pieces of paper which were reverently placed before the King, while the inundated Lord Melbourne received yet another plethora of letters, this time asking that the very people who had been partly to blame for the many complaints he had received during the last few months should be let off. The newspapers too, in London as well as Bristol, got into the act, using the trials and the results to beat the drum of Reform or Conservatism.

Bristolians were faced with a terrible dilemma during the second week of January, namely the choice of which trial to attend, for on the 9th, in the Merchants Hall (the meeting place of the Society of Merchant Venturers, founded in 1552 and still going strong today) fourteen officers assembled together under the presidency of Lieutenant-General Sir Henry Fane to hear eleven charges brought against Lieutenant-Colonel Thomas Brereton. The table at which the four major-generals, six colonels and four lieutenant-colonels sat in order of seniority ran down the centre of the room while there were two other tables at the sides, near the President's end: one was for Brereton to sit at (with Mr Earle of the Western Circuit, his counsel, and Mr Evans, his solicitor) and the other was where the evidence to be produced by the prosecution was laid out, bundled in red tape. Across one end of the room a barrier had been erected to keep back a thronging crowd, most of them upper and middle-class women — "The Thunderer", the London Times, reported that "part of the room was filled with ladies whose appearance and manner were in the highest degree prepossessing".

The Prosecutor was Major-General Sir Charles Dalbiac, who asserted that Brereton was guilty, collectively, of want of vigour and of highly disgraceful conduct prejudicial to good order and military discipline, the old catch-all phrase in military law which until the mid-20th Century was used to ensnare offenders when nothing else in the Manual of Military Law seemed appropriate. Specifically, Brereton was accused of: encouraging the rioters by temporising and being feeble;

withdrawing a troop of the 14th from Queen Square and then sending the whole detachment to Keynsham; falsely stating that the men and their horses were jaded and exhausted; refusing to recall them; refusing the order of the magistrates to protect the New Gaol; remaining inactive while the Bishop's Palace was being attacked; not endeavouring to extinguish the fire at the Mansion House and prevent its spreading; neglecting "to avail himself" of the Dodington Troop of Yeomanry; retiring to bed for several hours, notwithstanding having received a letter from the Mayor authorising him to take whatever steps he might consider necessary to restore and preserve the public peace; of being reluctant to send troops to Queen Square at 4 am on the Monday morning. . . . And, lastly, of improperly shaking hands and conversing with the rioters on various occasions during the 29th, 30th and 31st. To all these charges Brereton pleaded Not Guilty.

Major-General Dalbiac, long-nosed, bald-headed and aged about 55, was, like most of the court, a cavalryman. He was a crisp, matter-of-fact gentleman who had spent many a month fighting Napoleon's soldiers in the Peninsular, mostly with the 4th Light Dragoons, and had a logical mind and a lucid way of expressing himself. The scene was set for a fascinating public trial which got off to an interesting start when Ebenezer Ludlow said that Brereton had asked for a precise requisition from the magistrates before he would feel justified in opening fire but that the magistrates, whose authority the colonel never disputed, had not actually issued such a document because they naturally expected that the most effective measures would be adopted. . . .

In the Guildhall on Thursday the 12th of January five rioters were sentenced to be hanged while a quarter of a mile away the day's evidence before the Court Martial ended with Cornet Kelson saying that Brereton had told him that he had done the right thing by leaving the New Gaol with his small detachment of troopers even though the mob were in the process of setting fire to the place. Only five of the eleven charges had so far been dealt with by the prosecution: there was still a long way to go.

Dispirited, and appalled at the prospect of having to sit before all those goggling and contemptuous eyes, Brereton told his counsel that if he did not have to appear in court again he would plead Guilty to the rest of the charges, but when Mr Erle went to consult Captain Thompson, who was acting as Deputy Judge Advocate, he was told that Army Regulations stipulated that even when a prisoner pleaded Guilty it was the duty of the Court to hear all the evidence in order that they could make a proper judgement about the case and the sentence. Brereton, who normally retired to bed at ten pm every night, went to the Reeves hotel, dined with two friends and at about eleven pm was collected by his gardener in his gig and taken home to Redfield House at Lawrence Hill. He was not to appear in court again.

On the sixth day, January the 7th, Captain Lewis was brought before Mr Justice Bosanquet on the charge of killing young Thomas Morris. The case lasted only two days.

On Thursday the 12th of January the prisoners convicted of capital offences were brought before the judges to be sentenced and when that was finished the Commission then pronounced its work done.

The following Tuesday, the 17th of January, at one pm, the same military court convened to try Lieutenant-Colonel Brereton began the trial of Captain Warrington on three charges which were, in sum, that he "showed a want of vigour and activity which was unbecoming and disgraceful to his character as an officer, and calculated to bring dishonour on His Majesty's service". Captain Warrington apologised most sincerely for trespassing on the valuable time of the Court but asked that since this was the first time he had heard the charges would it be possible to postpone the proceedings until the 25th? The Court duly adjourned, reconvened eight days later, heard the last evidence on Thursday the 2nd of February and after deliberations in closed court, which lasted for several hours, sent their findings and recommendations to the King.

There was then a pause before it was confirmed that he had been found guilty, and an even longer pause before the final act of the Riots was put on public view, in London, not in Bristol, by the Trial of Charles Pinney, Esquire, late Mayor of Bristol, for neglect of duty. (In the interim, virtually nothing had been done to administer the affairs of the city.) He was arraigned before the Court of the King's Bench on Thursday the 25th of October 1832, almost exactly a year after the events which had led to his appearance before four judges and a jury consisting of twelve freeholders from the County of Berkshire. (John Hopkins, Esq, Foreman.) The Attorney General and the Solicitor General led for the Prosecution while Sir James Scarlett, three barristers and four solicitors acted as counsel for the Defence. (One of the solicitors was Mr Daniel Burges, the Mayor's clerk.) The trial lasted for six days, until the 31st of October.

In the intervening months more than six hundred people in Bristol had died of cholera, nearly half of those who caught it, and the Reform Bill had received the Royal Assent. It was now the law of the land and the long, slow road to greater equality could begin.

*

The Trial of Charles Pinney, Esq.
for neglect of duty

On October 25th 1832, at the Court of the King's Bench in London, upon information filed by the Attorney-General, Charles Pinney was brought to the bar.

"The avenues of the court were crowded at a very early hour by numbers of the most respectable persons who seemed to take the liveliest interest in the proceedings. The jury began to arrive at about nine o'clock and were the only persons admitted before the arrival of the judges except the gentlemen of the press, who received every accommodation from the officers of the Court. About ten o'clock Lord Tenterden, Mr Justice Littledale, Mr Justice Park and Mr Justice Taunton took their seats on the Bench. The doors were then thrown open and every part of the galleries and the body of the court was instantly crowded."

The information against Mr Pinney was that on the 29th October 1831, there being a riot in the city of Bristol, and the next day a riotous and tumultuous assemblage, the defendent, then being the Mayor of the said city and a Justice of the Peace, did not exert his authority to repress such outrage and omitted to give orders and to make such arrangements as were expedient and necessary.

The defendant pleaded Not Guilty.

The Attorney-General then rose and addressed the jury, saying that they were there to try an individual who had been placed in an office of trust but had betrayed that trust in that he, during nearly forty-eight hours, when Bristol, a city of the first rank in this great empire, was placed in a most alarming state of consternation and a situation of great danger, had neglected and abandoned his duty, and withdrawn from being found by those who wished to discover him. . . .

All magistrates were emphatically the conservators of the peace, the Attorney-General continued, called on by their office to exercise their authority to protect or restore the peace. After the riots of 1780 which occurred in consequence of Parliament having relaxed the laws against the Roman Catholics, the Lord Mayor of London had been charged with neglect of duty, (a similar case, where he had refused to read the Riot Act) brought to trial, convicted, but had died before sentence could be pronounced. . . .

Mr Pinney had been mistaken in the view he took of his duty for he seemed to have conceived that if he called in the aid of the military to put down the disturbance, and required them to act on their own responsibility, he altogether divested himself of authority and shifted it from his own shoulders to those of the military. Troops may act under their officers but it was desirable that they should always have the authority of the magistracy to conduct their proceedings. In this case the magistrates had repeatedly called on Lieutenant-Colonel Brereton and gave him a sort of commission to go out into the streets to exercise his authority, but they did not accompany him as they ought to have done. During the evening of the 29th of October, more than once, Colonel Brereton was required to clear the streets but could not get from the magistrates the specific orders to act which were necessary, and when he asked whether he should use violence to clear the streets he was told do it in any way he chose. . . .

The Mayor took no steps to gather the magistrates together the next morning, or to collect the civil force, or to make a plan for the suppression of the riot. Instead, there were debates and discussions, but nothing was done to secure the prisons from attack by the mob and Colonel Brereton was not called upon to direct his troops to the Bridewell and when Governor Humphries of the New Gaol asked what was to be done to defend it the Mayor said that if the mob were only to be appeased by releasing the prisoners, it might be as well to let them go — but the decision was up to him. . .!

During the afternoon of the Sunday, when a constable asked the Mayor if they could use firearms the Mayor informed him that it would be improper to do so, since if anyone was killed the constable might be tried for murder. That night, at the Recruiting Sergeant's office, the Mayor asked some of the soldiers how he could be protected, since he wished to escape — which he did, to Mr Fripp's house, at the very time when Colonel Brereton and Captain Codrington were looking for him. . . .

The next morning, when Major Beckwith asked the magistrates to accompany him on horseback to Queen Square they declined to do so, saying they could not ride — some that they had not been on horseback for eighteen years. (Laughter) When some gentlemen came to the magistrates and said they estimated that there were 800 guns in Bristol "Oh", said the magistrates, "you had better throw them in the Float!" (Much laughter.) When two Roman Catholic priests said they could find 200 sober Irishmen to join in the support of the law their offer was not accepted. In every instance where suggestions of that sort were made there was constant prevarication. The magistrates could and should have acted, but did not, and therein lay their neglect.

The Attorney-General then said he would call various witnesses and lay statements before the jury made by the Mayor himself in his letter of the 4th November to the Home Secretary, in which the circumstances were stated as strongly as possible against other people in order to find an excuse for the magistrates. He felt confident that after hearing the facts the jury would have no doubt that the Mayor was guilty of the charges against him.

John Newcombe was then called and examined by the Solicitor-General, as follows: A printer, residing at John Street. At four in the afternoon of the 29th was at the Mansion House, where there were more than fifty civil officers and a thousand or so people, of whom only fifty were rioters. Later the constables were drawn up by Major Mackworth and cleared the streets two or three times but the rioters returned soon after. The gas lights had been put out and the military said they could not see where they were riding so he was given a torch by the Mayor to carry before the soldiers. He left at about one o'clock. The number of civil officers had diminished by then; they had no direct orders to remain and when a dozen made a charge perhaps only seven came back. He went away because he was very fatigued from running before the soldiers with the light but returned to the Mansion House at about half past nine o'clock the next morning. It was in the possession of the mob, about 20 of them in the house, most of them intoxicated. He and a few others drove them out without difficulty. Later, witness saw Alderman Hilhouse and went with him to the side door where the Alderman read the Riot Act. There were then about 200 rioters assembled who immediately began to throw stones and glass bottles, which caused witness and the Alderman to retire within the Mansion House. Witness remained until half-past twelve, during which time the house was almost filled with respectable people. The Mayor was also there. The persons assembled offered to do all they could to quell the disturbance but the Mayor and the Alderman directed no force or staves to be used and enjoined them not to take anybody into custody. The people were to be persuaded to go home quietly. No attempt was made at this time to disperse the mob. Later, at the Guildhall at half-past three o'clock, when the citizens asked for authority to use firearms the Mayor and Aldermen refused, saying they must use their own discretion.

Cross-examined by Sir James Scarlett: When the soldiers arrived on the Saturday they were received with great cheering, many people crying out "The King and Reform", which was repeated by some of the soldiers. Many of the people were shaking hands with the soldiers. He took one of the officers of the 14th into the Mansion House who was wounded by his horse falling over the broken railings. The next day at the Guildhall he heard Sergeant Ludlow say to Colonel Brereton "In the King's name I command you to order the 14th instantly back to town" but Colonel Brereton persisted in his refusal. The Sergeant said he would report him for his refusal but later admitted that Colonel Brereton had given such reasons to the magistrates that they were satisfied it would be imprudent to bring back the 14th. He heard the colonel say that if they were brought back not a man of them would be left before the evening, and that the 3rd were so fatigued they were incapable of doing further duty. . . .

Witness had never heard anyone say "The Recorder ought to be led to a lamp post", nor that it would be better had he been thrown over the bridge: *after* the riots he had said that rather than such destruction having taken place it would have been better if the Recorder had been thrown over a bridge. . . . He knew the Bunch of Grapes but never said the words imputed to him there. He had refused to serve as a Special Constable for the protection of Sir Charles, but neither would he insult him or molest him in any way.

John Cossens, examined by Mr Sergeant Wilde: A straw manufacturer and Chief Constable of Castle Ward. The Sheriff, Mr Hare, had instructed each Ward to treble its forces. His number was nine and he raised eighteen more. Some had to be hired because people would not volunteer. On the Saturday they assembled at the Exchange at eight o'clock and were addressed by the Mayor, who said he was sorry to bring so many respectable persons from home, but though he did not believe there would be a riot did it as a precaution. He exhorted them to act with moderation. Mr Pinney had been present at a meeting connected with Reform; he was in favour of the Reform Bill, and so was everyone who was an honest man. (Laughter.). . .

There was a great deal of hissing and hooting and some stones were thrown in Temple Street and at the Guildhall. Later, at the Mansion House, the mob was throwing stones and breaking windows all the time. At four o'clock in the afternoon the mob was very riotous and the constables told the Mayor that if he did not send for the military the house would be down about their ears. Sir Charles Wetherell came up to witness and said there was not sufficient reason for the military to be sent for. Witness remained at the Mansion House till 12 o'clock at night, when all the constables were going home in various directions. They had been going gradually during the evening but no orders were given by any person for them to go or stop. . . .

At a little before 12 on the Sunday he went to Queen Square, where the mob were handing pitchers to the soldiers to drink. When he saw the mob hand in glove with the soldiers he though it prudent to go home as, being a constable, he was a marked character. At the end of Wine Street he saw Colonel Brereton with about twenty soldiers. The mob were cheering him and he had his cap off cheering them. He had no orders to act as constable until the next morning but at about ten o'clock in the evening saw Captain Codrington's troop arrive and told him that the mob had broken into wine vaults in Castle Street and taken liquors out. He begged the Captain for a few men to protect the property but the Captain said he could not act until he had heard the Riot Act read.

Samuel Waring, examined by Mr Sergeant Coleridge: A merchant, with a counting-house in King Street. At half past five o'clock in the evening of the 29th, hearing that there was a riotous mob in Queen Square, went there and saw a great number of persons around the Mansion House acting with violence and throwing stones. They then pulled down the rails and used them to break the windows with. He saw the mob break out the windows of the dining room and enter it with no resistance whatever offered to them. Saw two men take a bundle of straw into the Mansion House and ran to the city for the fire engines. He returned with a troop of the 3rd Dragoon Guards who were greeted by a cheer for the King. All rioting appeared to cease. . . .

Next morning at about a quarter before ten at Saint Augustine's Parade saw the Mayor, who appeared to be flurried. Witness left his carriage to speak to him. The

Mayor said he had just escaped from the Mansion House and entreated him to go to the Council House to see what could be done. Later, at the Guildhall, he suggested to the Mayor that some ruse might be practised to get the mob from the Mansion House; thought some effigy to attract them to Brandon Hill would answer the purpose. Witness did not recollect suggesting any effigy but as the mob were desirous of Sir Charles Wetherell, if he had suggested any effigy it would be his. (Laughter.). . .

Later, at the Mansion House, heard the mob say they were going to the Bridewell to release the prisoners taken there the night before. They went off one by one and he went to tell the magistrates what they were going to do. Alderman Hilhouse treated it very lightly. "Oh, never mind" he said, "the walls and gates are strong enough". Witness tried again to convince the Aldermen that assistance should be sent to the gaol but without success, and left the city and went home.

Thomas Sheppard, a corn factor residing in Queen Square. At eight o'clock on the 29th took his Staff, being a special constable, and went to the Mansion House to protect the magistrates. Found a number of constables but there was no arrangement amongst them. He saw the Mayor and proposed such a plan to him, who then asked Major Mackworth to form the constables into companies, which was done. Witness took command of a division of 25, at the corner of the Mansion House and had not been there 5 minutes when about a dozen of the 14th Dragoons came galloping past. He called out to know why they were retreating and the sergeant said they were not going to stay there to be murdered. One of the dragoons was severely wounded in the head. After this only five of his men stayed and so he went back into the Mansion House. No magistrate came down the stairs to give any orders, nor sent any. He was angry with the magistrates and said "Why don't you come down and expose yourselves to the fury of the mob as well as me?" He left the scene of confusion then as he was not supported. . . .

On the Sunday morning he saw about 200 persons, many of them children, attacking the Mansion House and no resistance was offered to them. The 14th Dragoons arrived between nine and ten o'clock. He saw Colonel Brereton go up and speak to them and they immediately rode away, the mob hooting and making a great noise. That night his house was burnt down but he passed through the mob frequently and was not at all meddled with. During the night no magistrate was there. . . .

Cross-examined: He heard Mr Pinney read the Riot Act on the Saturday night, but not when it was first read. Mr Pinney stood outside the Mansion House exposed to the mob. Mr Pinney was a little man, rather deformed; stones were thrown while he read the Riot Act. If the soldiers had had orders to fire the mob would soon have been dispersed.

Samuel Selfe, an ironmonger. On the Sunday went to the Bridewell and saw smoke rising from the part used as a prison. Then went to the New Gaol, where there was a great crowd. The gaol stands on an island. (The plan of the city of Bristol was here handed over to the jury, and the situation of the gaol was pointed out to them.) The only mode of access to the island was over swing bridges and they could readily have been turned to prevent persons getting to or leaving the island. Saw the mob of about 150, many of them women and boys, plunder the gaol, carrying away beds and cooking utensils. There were several thousand spectators on the island and an equal number on the other side. They might have amounted to five or ten thousand. Saw no magistrate there, nor did he observe any resistance offered to the plunderers. . . .

Went to Queen Square about ten o'clock. There was a great crowd there and the Mansion House was on fire. As various parts of it fell he heard cheers from the crowd. About thirty houses were set on fire in succession, the last about ten minutes before six o'clock when the soldiers arrived. A hundred or a hundred-and-fifty persons were engaged in pilfering houses. The robbers did not appear to be acting in a body; each appeared to be acting on his own account. (Laughter.) Twenty persons were engaged in burning and breaking open the houses, the rest in acts of plunder. There were no cheers when private property was destroyed.

James Townsend, a gardener, and occasional servant to Sheriff Lax. When the constables captured prisoners he more than once interfered with them for striking the prisoners after they had been taken into custody. A little after five, outside the Mansion House, received a blow which stunned him when attempting to gain access. Colonel Brereton assisted him to get in. Called for the magistrates but received no answer. Went into the room which had been occupied by Sir Charles Wetherell, and Mr Sheriff Bengough came from behind the State Bed. (Loud laughter.) Went into another bedroom upstairs and found several Aldermen there. (Laughter.) Went into a third bedroom and found two or three there also. (A laugh.). . .

Heard repeated orders given to Colonel Brereton to clear the streets but heard nothing said about firing. The colonel said the people were getting peaceable and he thought they would disperse in a short time. Saw two dragoons brought in wounded, and a constable at the same time. He was laid on a bed in the banqueting room. Saw Colonel Brereton in the streets shaking hands with the mob. Several of the magistrates sat up with the Mayor all night. The only person who went to bed was Mr Lax. Believed the Mayor went to bed on Sunday at the White Lion, in Broad Street. . . .

Witness remained with Mr Sheriff Lax during the night and left about seven in the morning. When he returned at 8 the mob were very violent. Several stones were thrown at him and he ran away to the Hole-in-the-Wall public-house, where he disguised himself in a sailor's dress and afterwards concealed himself in a corn loft. From that place got onto the leads of the Mansion House where he saw Mr Pinney on the leads of the larder with three or four female servants. (Laughter.) The female servants and his worship were making great efforts to get on the leads first and Mr Pinney said "For God's sake, young man, assist me". He leaned over and with the assistance of the females got the Mayor up. He asked which way he could escape and witness elevated him over the wall on his shoulders. . . .

Saw the Mayor again in the evening at the sheriff's house in Park Street. Asked the Mayor if he knew him, as he seemed afraid to trust him. He said he did not, but Mr Daniel said it was because witness was in a sailor's suit and that the Mayor would be quite safe, and that he was not to tell anyone where the Mayor was gone. Mr Daniel said the Mayor was going to Mr Fripp's in Berkeley Square. "I said I knew what he meant and I would not betray his worship. Various enquiries were made after he had gone but I did not tell anyone except Mr Sheriff Hare. . .".

Cross-examined: I gave up my situation with Mr Lax the day after a complaint was made against me. I was not dismissed. The complaint was for kissing the servant on the sofa. I am a Freeman of Bristol; the freedom having been conferred on me after the riots by the sheriff.

George Humphrey, clerk to Messrs Leman and Co. next door to the Mansion House. Between seven and eight on the Sunday morning saw the Mayor on the roof; was asked to get a ladder to assist him up. Procured the office ladder and he got into the house and asked for God's sake to show him out by any other way than the front door. Was taken into the garret where he escaped over the roof with Major Mackworth and some other gentlemen.

James Prowse, a surgeon. Saw the soldiers in front of the Mansion House on the Saturday evening; they appeared to be quite at their ease and were smoking and drinking. On the Sunday morning went to College Green where about 500 persons had assembled. The 14th Light Dragoons were there, stones were thrown by the mob and the soldiers fired several times. Five or six dragoons then came up and the crowd having given them a bottle of wine they went away. Saw them drinking with the mob on the quay.

Thomas M'Carthy, a stationer in Bridewell Lane. On the Sunday got on the roof of the prison from the back part of his premises and took the governor and his wife into his house. Went to the Guildhall and delivered the governor's message that the prison was attacked and the rioters intended to release the prisoners and set the gaol on fire. One of the gentlemen sitting at the table said "You say they have released the prisoners — pooh, pooh! that is all they can do". Humphries the gaoler came in at that time and said his prison was attacked and he wished to know what he was to do, was he to release the prisoners or defend the prison? Mr Alderman Hilhouse said they would give no directions but he must use his own discretion.

The Reverend Thomas Roberts, a Baptist Minister. On Sunday the 30th saw the Mayor and offered to speak to the mob and try to prevail on them to disperse, since he knew a great many of the lower orders. After deliberation with the magistrates the Mayor agreed. Went with three other men to Queen Square, where the mob appeared to be divided into two classes, one extremely riotous and drunk, the other, though of the same grade of society, laughing and enjoying the attack being made by the other party. Asked the military officer to make way for him to address the mob but the officer said it was useless to do so; the mob were perfectly harmless and on the best of terms with the military. Witness tried to address the mob but could not because of the noise and disturbance. Considered the mob to be chiefly composed of navigators. After he had been there about an hour most of the mob went away crying out "Bridewell, Bridewell!" (Note: "Navigators" were Irish labourers brought over to build the canal system in England, hence the word "navvy", used today as a description of a labouring man.)

Isaac Cook, a solicitor. On the Sunday afternoon went to the meeting called in the Guildhall at which the Mayor took the chair. Witness asked the Mayor what plan he had to propose and the Mayor said he had none. Mr Sergeant Ludlow rose and said every person must act on his own discretion. Witness asked the Mayor if he would allow eight or ten of the military to go with him and try to get rid of the mob but the Mayor said he had no power over the military. When he asked the Mayor who had, he replied the military commander, of course. Witness then expressed surprise that he had not been summoned to such a meeting whereupon the Mayor said he would immediately send for Colonel Brereton. He did so, and on his arrival he was taken into a private room with the magistrates. When he came out he said the men were too tired and could not go. Witness then said "I see the city is given up to destruction".

Cross-examined: Witness knew the necessity for the co-operation of the military because from his experience in 1800 he knew what a Bristol mob was.

John Keagan, floor-cloth manufacturer. At a quarter before six on the Sunday evening was with 20 or 30 persons in the Guildhall when the Mayor addressed them. He said "Gentlemen, we have come to no decision. I will do anything you can devise with the exception of calling in the military. They have rendered themselves obnoxious by firing upon the populace contrary to orders and I am confident that if they were called in again every one of them would be sacrificed before morning. I will do anything you wish except call in the 14th for I do not wish to endanger the life of any person."

The Reverend Francis Edgeworth, a Catholic priest. Was in Queen Square during the afternoon and evening of Sunday, 30th. At eight, the mob removed the door of the cellar to the Mansion House, about 20 persons entered and a large barrel of liquor was brought out by a man or boy. At ten a much larger number entered the front of the house and started to break up the floor with axes, even though six or seven dragoons were outside. A boy of about 13 urged people to go up the stairs but finding no-one followed him said "Why don't you come on, are you scared?", which was received with a sort of cheer and the mob followed him up, chiefly lads about 16. After a short period of looting the place was set on fire. Saw Colonel Brereton ride into the Square with 10 or 20 dragoons. The colonel asked the soldiers who had been on duty how it was the Mansion House had been set in flames and when the soldiers answered "How could we help it?" replied "My lads, don't fire," and riding forward among a large number of people importuned them to leave.

Benjamin Green, an accountant. In consequence of being told in church on Sunday that all able-bodied men should attend upon the magistrates that afternoon at the Guildhall he went there. A little after four o'clock Colonel Brereton arrived and said that his men had been on duty for thirty hours, their horses were unable to pick their heels up one after the other and must have refreshment.

William Platts, Staff-Sergeant clerk in the Recruiting Office. Was on duty on the Sunday when the Mayor and five or six gentlemen arrived. They appeared agitated and asked if there was a means of escape out of the back. Colonel Brereton was at the Adjutant's quarters across the Green but had left orders to be sent for if anyone enquired for him. The Mayor said they did not want him. A gentleman wrote a letter at the Mayor's dictation. Mr Pinney then asked witness to go and get any sort of old greatcoat and pair of trousers from Mr Osborne in Lower Green, which he did. Colonel Brereton then came in, witness having told him the Mayor and other gentlemen were there. The Mayor stayed until eight but returned in about an hour.

Cross-examined. It had been raining very hard and the gentlemen were very wet. He could not tell for which gentleman the coat and trousers were.

The statements to Lords Melbourne and Hill by the Mayor were then put in and read to the Court, after which Captain Codrington was called:

After arriving on the Sunday evening met Colonel Brereton, who was in his uniform, and asked him where he was likely to find a magistrate. The colonel said he would take him if he had a horse. Witness procured one and they went looking for two magistrates but could not find any at home. Witness said he believed the Riot Act had been read several times, to which the colonel replied that it was nothing to do with him. He then suggested his lieutenant should take off his coat and read the Riot Act but the colonel replied "That won't do". Witness suggested the colonel should take his troop to Queen Square, but the colonel said that would not do either. Witness proposed joining the 14th, to which the colonel replied "They are gone, sir, they are gone; we have sent them out of town or there would not have been one of them left alive".

Major Beckwith, Commandant of the 14th Light Dragoons: On arriving at the Council House the magistrates complained that Colonel Brereton had not supported them and that the mob were in complete possession of the city. He asked for three or four magistrates to accompany him on horseback and he would soon restore order. They all refused. Witness then asked them individually but they all refused, one saying it would make him unpopular, another that it would cause his shipping to be destroyed. They all said none of them knew how to ride on horseback (laughter) except Mr Alderman Hilhouse, who said he had not been on horseback for 18 years and would hold anyone responsible who said he could ride. Witness then said he would require a written authority to adopt such measures as he might think expedient to put down the riots, and when he had got this asked the Mayor to accompany him. He said if he did so his shipping or his property would be destroyed. When his soldiers of the 14th arrived back in town Witness led several charges at full speed. Colonel Brereton several times came up and sat on his horse doing nothing, saying it was impossible to quell the riot.

Cross-examined. Witness had not said that the Mayor had been unjustly blamed and he would take care the saddle was put on the right horse, but he had no doubt of saying that he thought it unjust to throw all the blame on the magistrates and the Mayor.

The Attorney-General, having called in all 33 witnesses, stated that this was the case for the Prosecution.

Sir James Scarlett rose for the Defence and addressing the jury at great length said, amongst many other things, that the Mayor and magistrates had suffered much persecution and misrepresentation, and that for the twelve months since the riots occurred they had been subjected to a secret investigation by a private committee of their own townsmen, composed largely of that party which was opposed to the magistracy. . . .

This was, he said, one of the most important cases ever to come before this great tribunal, for if the Mayor of Bristol could be convicted on the evidence laid before them there would be no safety for any magistrate in the kingdom. No honesty, no zeal, no integrity could save him from the malice or vengeance of his enemies. . . .

Parts of his Learned Friend's statement had been contradicted by the evidence. The whole of it could be summed up in two sentences, namely: that all the efforts made by the magistrates to induce Colonel Brereton to use his exertions to suppress the riot were totally ineffectual, and, secondly, that in consequence of the military refusing to suppress the riot the civil force of Bristol also refused to aid the magistrates. That really was the general state of the case laid before the jury by the Prosecution and upon that they were required to hold them responsible for the burning of the town. . . .

Could anybody doubt, Sir James asked, that if on the Saturday the magistrates had ordered the military to fire when an officer had said "I can't fire", and that life had been taken away, that the magistrates would have been indicted for murder?

Sir James then delivered a scathing attack upon Mr Goss, calling him a trouble-making speech maker who bullied the magistrates and made a great deal of trouble because his foolish plan (to issue the guns in the city to responsible inhabitants who could then form themselves into companies for the protection of the city) had not been adopted. . . .

The jury had heard that although the whole mob of persons did not join in the plundering, yet by their cries and shouts they encouraged those who did; that such was the apathy of the inhabitants that the magistrates could not put down the plunderers, with shouts of "The King and Reform" proceeding from 10,000 people. . . .

As regards the evidence of Townsend, the discharged servant, the jury were called upon to believe that the Mayor had made a ridiculous escape. He would prove to them by three or four reliable witnesses that there was not a word of truth in that story. . .

"We are told" Sir James continued, "that in Constantinople, where the mobs govern the Sultan, it sometimes obliges him to throw them out a Prime Minister to work their pleasure upon; and so perhaps Mr Waring, the Quaker, with whom it was a matter of religion not to give a direct answer on cross-examination, and not to take off his hat, might have said to the magistrates "Just throw out Sir Charles Wetherell to the mob. The insulted feelings of the former will be appeased by tearing him to pieces, and all will be quiet." Indeed one of the witnesses did express a wish that Sir Charles had been thrown into the river, but I am sure you would not have approved of the magistrates pursuing either that or Mr Waring's plan. . ."

At the time of the riots troops were required in various parts of the country and probably a greater number could not be spared, in the first instance, than were sent to Bristol. "I am not instructed to complain of the deficiency of the force, or to blame the conduct of Colonel Brereton," Sir James said. "That officer acted under a fearful responsibility and if it could after have been shown that there were means of preserving the town without violence he might have been made to answer — and maybe he acted under that impression — for any blood that might have been shed. He would have been guilty of murder if he had ordered the troops to fire, even if ordered to do so by the magistrates, if it had been his deliberate conviction that such a measure was unnecessary in consequence of the good humour of the crowd. It is proved that Colonel Brereton stated to the magistrates that he had insufficient force, considering the inhabitants would not come forward to support them, and that he must gain time and send in all directions for reinforcements (which was done) and that by Monday he would be strong enough to suppress the riot. . . ."

Despite the fact that on the Sunday handbills were produced and distributed all over the city only 200 men out of at least 30,000 able-bodied men responded to the call to assist the magistrates. Many of the constables who had been on duty the night before had been wounded. Consider, gentlemen, Sir James went on, what a destitute situation the magistrates were placed in. . . .

On the Sunday evening when the Mayor had to leave the Recruiting Office because the mob were returning he was told he had better go to Clifton but he refused, saying he would not leave the town. This despite the fact that he was much fatigued and had had no sleep and no food since the Saturday morning. He could not have gone to the Council House without danger to his life but he made known to the civil and military authorities where he was during the night.

As to his guilt, Sir James said, does the Attorney-General say he was guilty of being absent from his post? Where was that post? Was he a criminal because he went to lie down for an hour? Was he guilty because he failed to call out the military? His own witnesses have withdrawn that ground from under him. Was he guilty in not calling out the Posse Comitatus sooner? If so, I think you will have no doubt it is a work that cannot be accomplished in a moment. . ..

"If magistrates are to be convicted upon evidence such as that offered to you, I declare before God in Heaven that justice can no longer exist in this country. I beg your pardon, gentlemen, for having troubled you at such length but I did it becuse I felt it my duty to defend the magistrates. They have exposed their wives, their families, their fortunes and their lives, and what is their reward? This is only the first step; there are nine other informations. I shall now present the evidence."

With that, Sir James sat down, having spoken for nearly eight hours.

The first witness for the Defence, William Hare, Under-Sheriff, gave an account of the arrival of Sir Charles Wetherell, of the measures taken to hire extra constables, most of whom were members of the Bristol Political Union and were paid at the rate of 3s.6d. per day, compared to the 4s. per day paid to the regular constables. Mr Hare said that Mr Pinney was a popular man who took the chair at a meeting to celebrate The three days of Paris.

Daniel Burges, city solicitor and clerk to the Mayor. Stood near the Mayor when he read the Riot Act. A stone cut through witness' hat, which very much hurted his head, and a brickbat hit his side so severely as almost to deprive him of breath. The Mayor showed no terror or alarm but acted with the greatest fortitude. He would not admit that he was exhausted but appeared to the witness to be so. During the Sunday evening a report came in that the shipping had been set on fire but the Mayor showed no fear whatever. In Colonel Brereton's room at the Recruiting Office two sergeants came in stating "They are caught; they are caught like a rat in a trap". When the mob came back witness went towards the Green, where a man ran by waving a cudgel shouting "F. . . the flaming Bishops, down with the Bishops!" How the Mayor escaped he could not tell; he thought all their lives were in danger by staying there. Later, he went back to find the colonel but a man on the door would not let him enter and appeared to be drunk. . . . During the whole of Saturday, Sunday and Monday morning the Mayor had not shown anything like personal fear. It was impossible for a man to conduct himself with more firmness and propriety than the Mayor did.

Cross-examined. Witness did not hear the Mayor say he considered Colonel Brereton's office a place of safety. Saw a sentinel there but did not hear the Mayor ask for one to be placed there to give timely notice of the approach of the mob. He had known Mr Pinney for many years but had never seen him riding a tall horse.

Mr Sergeant Ludlow, Town Clerk. Had been so from 19 to 20 years. Gave Colonel Brereton directions to disperse the mob and clear the streets. Previous to that Colonel Brereton had said the mob was in a good humour and he could disperse them by merely riding the troops about. He said it at least twenty times during the course of the evening. On the Sunday morning, when the troops fired and a shot struck the church very near to where he was standing, several persons told him it was a great shame Sir Charles Wetherell had been brought to town. Witness said Sir Charles had as good a right to hold his opinions as they did. They said he had better be careful what he said, he was as bad as Sir Charles. . . .

During the afternoon a proposition was made that fresh horses should be provided for the troops since theirs were knocked up but the colonel said it was no use putting dragoons on untrained horses. Many people had said the colonel was a traitor and a coward and at the time witness had been inclined to lean to that view of him but he now thought him sincere, and that he wished to give time to relieve his troops. That evening he had gone to borrow a coat and trousers, being wet through with the rain and afraid to carry an umbrella as everyone was knocked down who had one. Stayed at Mr Osborne's just long enough to put on dry clothes, eat two mutton chops and drink a glass of wine and water. (Laughter.) When told the mob were at the Bishop's Palace the colonel had said "We must not delay any longer but have the men out" — meaning the 3rd Dragoon Guards. . . .

During all this time the Mayor did all in his power and never took consideration for his personal safety.

Major Digby Mackworth, aide-de-camp to Lord Hill. Had been 20 years on the Ordnance staff. On the Saturday, when the Mayor gave the order to use the utmost force to put the riot down Colonel Brereton asked, "Am I to fire, sir?" The Mayor paused and then said "You must fire if the riot cannot be suppressed without". Witness then begged the Mayor and Colonel Brereton not to fire, saying that firing was a bad mode for cavalry to adopt and that shots meant for rioters might hit innocent people. Witness suggested that if the constables were organised properly they might answer the purpose.

Witness had never seen the Mayor show any want of personal courage; indeed he was, perhaps, the most cool of the party. He could not have done more by any means than the Witness saw. There were no women present when the Witness and the Mayor made their escape over the leads of several houses, until they reached a window in the Custom House which was opened by a woman.

On the Monday morning in Queen Square Witness had ordered the dragoons to charge without obtaining permission from Colonel Brereton. He made several charges and the colonel charged with him. He had begged his pardon for ordering the charge but said he could not help it because of the extreme urgency of the case.

Cross-examined. The constables were in the most disorganised state. He fancied that several persons he saw escaping were special constables. Was so disgusted with the party feeling that existed in Bristol, shown especially during the discussions in the Guildhall, that he left the city on the Sunday evening determined to do nothing until the next morning.

Re-examined by Sir James Scarlett: Went amongst the people to ascertain their feelings. Some said all was right, others that they were for the King and Reform. On the Monday the troops who had been pelted out of the city were welcomed by the lower orders with delight and joy. Witness had no opportunity to discover any military talent in the Aldermen of Bristol. To put firearms in the hands of the constables would have been most impolitic.

William Harmer, an attorney. On the Sunday morning, while the mob were shouting "The King" and "Reform" one man shook Colonel Brereton by the hand; the colonel said "I am for Reform, my lads, as well as you". The mob exclaimed against the 14th and said: "We will murder the bloody Blues." The colonel said he would send them out of town and the mob then cheered him and said he was a good fellow. Witness saw the 3rd Dragoons drinking repeatedly with the mob. Saw a bottle thrown at one of the 14th which hit him on the back of the head. When the man presented his pistol at the man Colonel Brereton struck his arm up. . . .

That evening at the Bishop's Palace witness attempted to rescue some property and had a sword in his hand. Colonel Brereton said "Put up that sword or I will cut you down". Witness was very angry, partly because he had seen the troops make way for persons to pass through with plunder in their hands. Witness cut at a plunderer with his sword and a soldier said "You have already been told to put up that weapon, sir, and if you do not I will cut you down". When the bishop's butler refused to let go of a man a soldier struck at him with his sword and cut his nose. The prisoner then got away.

The Reverend James Bulwer. After officiating at Clifton church on Sunday went to Bristol and heard many respectable people say the riots served the Corporation right for bringing that arrant villain Sir Charles down to insult the inhabitants of Bristol. At the tollgate while it was being destroyed a mechanic said that if it were not for the boroughmongering Lords there would be enough for all but as it was they took the bread out of the mouths of people and then sent the soldiers to shoot them.

Isambard Kingdom Brunel, a civil engineer. Assisted in trying to suppress the riots. Was at the Mansion House and the Palace when they were attacked. The whole of the Saturday the multitude shouted and encouraged the mob. On the Monday he observed a great number of the special constables whom he had observed the day before as actively engaged in the riots.

James Gibbons, clerk. Saw the Mayor make his escape on the Sunday morning and swore there was no female present at the time.

On the Sixth Day of the Trial, Sir James Scarlett closed the case for the Defence, having called, in all, twenty witnesses. The Attorney-General then rose to reply.

He said that Sir James Scarlett, who had succeeded Sir Charles Wetherell in office, in a peroration marked more by labour than eloquence, had sought to cast imputations at those who had felt it their duty to bring this case. He charged the Mayor with dereliction of duty throughout the period from Saturday morning until Monday morning and asked the jury whether it would be possible for the Government to face the people of England if they had failed to call for an inquiry into the conduct of the magistrates, who had themselves called for a Court of Inquiry and a Court Martial to investigate the conduct of the military.

The charge against the magistrates could be divided into three: first, general desertion of duty; secondly, general non-interference in cases where immediate and active interference should have taken place and thirdly, the Mayor's conduct. He then went on to say that while he was most happy to accept that the imputations of the Mayor's cowardice and misconduct were now fully disproved — he had displayed the highest courage and spirit — he could not clear him of having deserted his official responsibilities. He charged the magistrates with having failed to accept responsibility, with having formed no plans and exercised no authority.

In the opinion of the Attorney-General the unwilling-
ness of Colonel Brereton to have recourse to the sword,
when he thought the sacrifice of life to be useless, was
quite justifiable. In facing the enemy Colonel Brereton
would have felt no hesitation but he did feel hesitation in
exposing uselessly the lives of his own men, and cutting
down his fellow citizens. He was glad they had heard
tardy justice rendered to his fame and honour.

He was confident that the case for the prosecution had
been fully made out and that public justice required the
jury to declare the magistrates guilty of great and unwar-
rantable neglect in the performance of their duties.

The Court adjourned at a few minutes before six
o'clock on the 31st October 1832. The next day, Lord
Tenterden having been indisposed for two days and
remaining so, the three judges came into court, having
held a consultation with several Judges belonging to the
other Common Law Courts of the King's Bench Cham-
ber. Mr Justice Littledale summed up.

It was for the jury to consider what had occurred and
decide whether Mr Pinney had, under all the circumstances in which he was placed, faithfully discharged his
duty. The jury, or many of them, were probably magistrates and were therefore able to decide what a magistrate was expected to do on such an occasion. It
appeared that there was considerable apathy on the part
of the inhabitants of the city of Bristol and no great
disposition to suppress the riots. The Learned Judge
then went through each of the charges against the Mayor
in series and concluded that in his opinion it was impossible to substantiate a charge of neglect against him. He
concluded his summing up, which had taken two hours
and twenty minutes to deliver, by saying that if the jury
were of the opinion that he had neglected his duty in any

one particular they would find him guilty; if not, they would acquit him.

The other Judges concurred entirely with the summing up of the Learned Brother.

The jury retired at a quarter before one and on their return at ten minutes past the Foreman stated that they had unanimously found Charles Pinney Not Guilty. Their verdict was received with expressions of approbation from the friends of the late Mayor.

A Gentleman wished to know from their Lordships whether they were to have their "expences" for having been detained in town for nine days. Mr Justice Littledale said he could give no directions on that point. Mr Justice Park observed that he did not know if the Attorney-General intended to proceed with the other indictments.

The Attorney-General stated that he had no intention to announce at present whether he should proceed with them or not. The gentlemen, however, if they wished it, might leave town.

*

When the news of the acquital of the late Mayor reached Bristol it was received with great joy, and the church bells were rung in celebration. The other indictments were not proceeded with.

The Commanding Officer called to Account

The headquarters of the Society of Merchant Venturers was their Hall, in King Street, near the Broad Quay and only a two minute walk from Queen Square. Originally the chapel of St Clement, it had been a small and unpretentious building until, between 1719 and 1722, a new Great Room was built and a "handsome way" was erected at the entrance, with ornamental railings, heavily scrolled iron gates and an elaborate and imposing facade above it — at a total cost of £1,000. Towards the end of the century further extensive work was done, for the large sum of £6,000, which included the installation of some splendid lamps and chandeliers. (These set the Merchants back £542 which, interestingly, was the equivalent of twenty labouring men's wages for a year then but today, at around £22,000, would pay wages for only five men's work for half a year at the current average wage of £178 per week.)

The Great Room in which the Court Martial took place was as imposing as the outward appearance of the building. Tall and well-proportioned, its huge entrance doors and fireplaces were framed by Corinthian capitals surmounted by classical arches embellished with a touch of the Baroque. From the moulded ceiling hung two of the chandeliers, in the Dutch style but double-tiered, and at one end there was a magnificent gilt-framed mirror twelve feet high.

Along the length of a large table down the middle of the room sat the fourteen officers who were members of the Court, while at the head of the table sat the President, Lieutenant-General Sir Henry Fane, and the lowly Captain, Thompson of the 81st of Foot, who had been appointed Deputy Judge Advocate. All of them, except Colonel Forster of the Royal Artillery, wore scarlet; he was in blue, with heavy, gold-braided epaulettes. Many of the officers wore campaign medals from the Napoleonic Wars, and the generals displayed the stars of noble Orders which had been conferred upon them for exemplary service.

To the left of the President, at a separate little table, sat the accused, Lieutenant-Colonel Thomas Brereton, also in scarlet but with a high blue "choker" collar embellished with silver piping, which was also sewn in twisted cords across the front of his tunic. He had brown hair, and a good head of it; cut short and not swept back it fell across his forehead in a way which could not have changed much since he was a boy. The table was covered with brown baize and on it was a pewter ink-stand and pot, quill pens and parchment for the use of his learned counsel. The chairs in the room were all of a kind; expensive mahogany dining-chairs with velvet seats (the place was used, among other things, for the Venturers' banquets). A tall writing desk was placed behind the prisoner's table for the use of the gentlemen of the press: the reporters from the London Times, the Bristol Mercury, the Journal, the Gazette and the rest.

Crowded in on all these people were the "ton" of the city. Perhaps two hundred people were there, crammed into the doorways and standing on chairs to get a glimpse of what was going on. At least half of them were women, wearing the fussy fashions of the day: high-waisted, heavily-draped silk and velvet dresses, and coats made from great swathes of material, with voluminous sleeves and trimmed with fur or lace collars. On their heads each and every one had a poke bonnet, the craze for which was at its height: great projecting brims, fashioned with lace or embroidery, framed pert or raddled faces around which curls and ringlets peeped. They carried muffs and velvet handbags and watched with uncomprehending avidity, not taking in what was going on or understanding its significance but inwardly digesting for future gossip the scene before them: the way their friends were dressed and how elegant the men looked in their fur-trimmed cloaks, high collars, frilled shirts and silken stocks. But for all the splendour of the scene because baths were not indulged in to any great extent in those days, even by the wealthy (the poor bathed not at all), there must have been a somewhat fetid atmosphere, ameliorated only by the ladies' perfumes.

The Court met at ten o'clock on the morning of the 9th of January and the President began by saying that in order to save time any questions which members of the Court wanted to put to witnesses by way of cross-examination should be written on slips of paper and then handed to the Judge Advocate, who would read them out. The charges were then read to the prisoner and to each Lieutenant-Colonel Brereton stood and replied "Not Guilty". The Deputy Judge Advocate then read out the list of witnesses who would be called and told them to withdraw from the room or they would not be permitted to give evidence. General Sir Charles Dalbiac, the Prosecutor, then addressed the Court.

He said that some of the charges carried a degree of cupability unprecedented in the character of a British officer. The Bristol Riots, with their consequences, had been discussed by all parties. Some had ascribed them to one cause, some to another. Some fixed the blame on the civic authorities, others on the military but all agreed that in some quarter or another there was great and unquestionable culpability. The intensity of interest excited by the present trial was such as had rarely been equalled in matters put before a military tribunal. Never, he believed, was there a case in which the leading facts and circumstances were less perfectly known or less distinctly understood. . . .

Because the testimony produced would relate to circumstances which took place over a period of three days and two nights of almost incessant disorder and alarm it was to be expected that there would be discrepancies in questions of time and other subordinate matters. However, he anticipated no difficulty in reconciling those variations on every essential point.

The General then told the assembled throng that he felt he was not up to the onerous task placed upon him. He had considered asking to be excused of it but had refrained from doing so because of the principle which had uniformly prompted him throughout a long professional life; namely never to shrink from any duty which the King might graciously think proper to impose on him. He would therefore execute the duties of Prosecutor to the best of his humble abilities. He confidently anticipated the indulgence of the Court for any want of skill he might show, and still more confidently the wonted clemency of their most gracious Monarch. . . .

There was one circumstance in the case from which he derived the most unspeakable relief — a circumstance which rarely befell the Prosecutor in a General Court Martial — namely the fact that he had not the slightest tinge of prejudice or partiality towards the prisoner at the bar. . . .

The General then detailed the circumstances of the outrages insofar as they were concerned with the operations of troops under Colonel Brereton's command, and concluded by saying that if his anxiety to discharge his duty might occasionally betray him into earnestness in pressing home the evidence against the prisoner, he beseeched Colonel Brereton to ascribe his urgency to zealous devotion to the service of His Majesty, and a deep solicitude for the honour of their profession. He hoped the prisoner would acquit him of any motive as unworthy as hostility towards himself.

The first witness was then called:

Mr Sergeant Ludlow said he had been unacquainted with the prisoner before the 29th October. (When asked by the prosecutor who had commanded the troops called out that evening he said he presumed they were commanded by Lieutenant-Colonel Brereton.) The colonel, he said, had been told to disperse the mob, clear the streets and get the city quiet as soon as possible but in his opinion that had not been done as promptly and effectually as it should have been. . ... The colonel had repeatedly said that the mob were very good humoured and he could walk them away by merely riding the horses about. When two wounded dragoons were brought in, one of them severely, he asked the colonel if these were symptoms of good humour — and if he had instructions which prevented him from doing as the magistrates ordered. He said he had not, and the witness then told him his orders were to clear the streets. The troops then drove the mob out of the green part of the square but they retired to the courts and passages in front of the houses.

Mr Ludlow continued: "An officer, I think in blue, came in and asked for permission to fire on people who had taken refuge on boats which could not be reached by the soldiers but Alderman Daniel said a great many of them were market boats with traders on board who should not be injured. Colonel Brereton then said "If you take my advice you will let them alone. It is getting very late and I dare say they will go quietly home to bed". He said troops would patrol the city during the night and he would be answerable for its peace. The square was clear at the time that Ludlow left it, he said, or he should not have withdrawn.

Cross-examined by the Court: Colonel Brereton said, once or twice, "If I am to fire I must have an explicit order". "I am not aware that such an order was given, in my presence." (The Prosecutor here admitted that Colonel Brereton did receive the sanction of the magistrates not to fire on a particular occasion when he referred to them.) When asked if the magistrates accompanied the troops in the streets in the suppression of rioting Mr Ludlow replied: "I have no personal knowledge of that fact."

Charles Pinney Esq told the Court that he was the Mayor and that when Colonel Brereton asked if he was to fire on the crowd he was told he should if it was necessary, or words to that effect. The colonel had not been restricted by him from the application of the edge of the sword. . ... At one time the colonel came in and said that because of the good temper of the mob his arm was tired from shaking hands with them. "He protested against using force in my presence," the Mayor went on, "saying it was unneccesary, and if it was used the responsibility would be ours". After orders were given to put down the riot the violence increased. He understood a charge had been made but he did not see it.

Colonel Brereton declined to cross-examine the witness.

Cross-examined by the Court: "I am under the impression I told him the Riot Act had been read. He must have known it from its being the subject of conversation in the room." In his opinion the colonel's conduct, especially the familiarity with which he treated the mob, must have given confidence to the rioters. The colonel gave the impression of being feeble and temporising.

There were no civil authorities in the streets acting in concert with the troops. None of the magistrates left the Mansion House to go with the troops when they were ordered to clear the streets. "I believe Colonel Brereton understood that he was to fire and use the edge of the sword if it was necessary," Mr Pinney said.

Captain Gage of the 14th Light Dragoons told the Court that his troop was ordered to load by Colonel Brereton while they were in quarters and did so. When the troop first arrived in the square at a quick trot violence ceased, but after they were ordered to clear the streets, at about eleven o'clock, it increased. They were ordered to disperse the mob without drawing swords or using violence. Three or four of his troopers were badly cut by stones and pieces of iron thrown by rioters. Witness went into the Mansion House and asked leave of the Mayor to use carbines on rioters who were pelting the soldiers. The Mayor hesitated for some time but was about to grant it when Colonel Brereton, in the doorway at the top of the stairs, recommended that it should not be done. They then cleared the mob, except for those who got into the boats and barges, and were about to go home to feed the troops and be relieved by the second troop of the squadron when they were told to go to the Council House by Colonel Brereton.

The group with which the Captain patrolled Wine Street were very much annoyed by being pelted with stones and pieces of iron, especially by a mob in an alley who were led by a man in a light-coloured dress who always advanced a few paces into the street before he threw a missile. The third or fourth time he did it the captain drew his pistol and levelled it at him but it snapped, and so the soldier on his left fired. The man fell. After that the mob left the passage and they were no more pelted by them. That occupied till half-past twelve. He then took part of the troop off, leaving Lieutenant Dawson and the Sergeant Major with the rest to patrol the streets on the understanding that they would be relieved in two hours.

Sergeant Edward Deane of the 3rd Dragoon Guards said that with respect to the colonel shaking hands with the rioters, he always supposed it was against the colonel's consent.

The Prosecutor here announced that the evidence in support of the first charge was closed and that the witnesses in respect of the second, third and fourth charges would be called as if they were one, they being so blended together in point of fact.

Mayor Pinney: On the Sunday, when Lieutenant-Colonel Brereton came to the Guildhall he refused to recall the 14th, saying it would bring about their certain destruction. The colonel turned down all the suggestions made by the Town Clerk, namely that the horses be rested by degrees, the troops put on fresh horses, or that they should act on foot. Colonel Brereton had not, to his knowledge, applied for the magistrates to accompany him with the troops to put down the riots.

Alderman Hilhouse, asked if he had given orders for the troops to fire to disperse the rioters on the Sunday morning, could not swear that he had done so, but each time after reading the Riot Act, which he did three times, he told the crowd the troops would fire if they did not disperse. When Colonel Brereton came up he told him the troops must clear the square; the colonel replied that cavalry carbines were not like infantry muskets, the troops had been up all night and were much fatigued, and that they were not equal to dealing with the mob. He said they must keep the mob in good humour and endeavour to get the troops rested, or else by evening the city would be given up to plunder and slaughter. He complained that the mob were infuriated because the 14th had shot a man the night before; shortly after he sent them away. That afternoon he refused to bring them back, saying that if he did there would not be a man of them alive the next morning.

Questioned by the prisoner: Did not Colonel Brereton, in the presence of Robert Marshall, request you to give orders to fire, and did you not refuse to give orders to fire? — I never heard any such request, nor did I refuse to give orders to fire.

Was not the Bedminster Troop of Yeomanry in Bristol throughout the whole of Sunday, with the Mayor's knowledge, and was the fact never communicated to Colonel Brereton? — I never knew they were in Bristol.

William Harmer, said he saw Colonel Brereton riding on to the Green on the Sunday morning followed by several boys and men who were using very gross expressions such as "Down with the bloody Blues" and "We'll murder the bastards". Colonel Brereton said "I am going to send the 14th out of town". Later, when he said this to the mob in Queen Square they cheered.

Captain Gage described the retreat from the square to the Green, during which his men fired at the mob, and then said that in his opinion his men were capable of performing any duty which cavalry could be called upon to perform at the time when they were sent out of Bristol.

Corporal Smith, of the 3rd Dragoon Guards, said that the colonel took off his cap in front of the mob and said "For God's sake, my good fellows, go home", to which the answer was they would not go until the 14th had been sent away. The colonel asked if they would disperse if he did, and they said yes they would, and then gave a huzza for the King and Reform. Shortly after the 14th went threes left and marched off.

John Johnson, a blacksmith, said he had seen Colonel Brereton make his obeisance to the lowest of the low, taking off his hat and shaking the hands of the mob.

Cornet Kelson said he was ordered by Lieutenant-Colonel Brereton to take his detachment of twenty men of the 3rd Dragoons to the New Gaol at half-past three on the Sunday afternoon. He asked the colonel what he was to do when he got there and the colonel said he could give him no orders to act; he could find no magistrate to give him any orders. "I was on no account to use any violence but to go there and return. There was an immense mob there. I marched the men up to the gate then put them threes about and took them back to College Green. The colonel asked me what I had done and I said I had done what he told me — nothing. He said he heard I had shot four men there and I replied I had done nothing of the sort. He told me I had acted perfectly right."

Questioned by the prisoner: Did you tell Lieutenant-Colonel Brereton that you found ten thousand rioters there and you could do nothing against them, and that you could not find any magistrate or civil authority there? I recollect telling Lieutenant-Colonel Brereton that I saw an immense mob at the gaol, destroying it, and that I had done nothing to check them, but I do not recollect saying anything about magistrates.

The Court then adjourned, having so far heard, in all, the evidence of twenty witnesses.

*

On the fifth day, Friday the 13th at two o'clock, the Court reassembled and, their names having been called over, the President immediately stood and said "You will probably have heard a most distressing report relative to the prisoner. I have sent Major Mackworth and the District Surgeon to ascertain the facts and if you please we must wait to hear the report of these individuals."

Shortly after this Major Mackworth entered the room "covered in dirt". The President then addressed him thus:

"Major Mackworth, in conformity with the order you received have you been to the house of Colonel Brereton?"

"I have."

"Was he dead or alive?"

"He was dead."

*

The Court was adjourned, having had an appropriate entry made in the minutes. General Dalbiac then addressed those present, saying that if the news had caused pain to the Court how much more pain it must have caused to the individual assigned the task of Prosecuting. He had a degree of distress and embarrassment such as he never remembered feeling in the course of his whole life. He had but one consolation, that he had entered the court without the slightest tinge of prejudice against the prisoner. He had never met him before the

17th November, when he had been put in charge of the Court of Inquiry, but had he been a sworn friend and brother officer instead of a stranger he would not have departed from his duty.

Sir Charles delivered this address "in a most feeling manner and sat down much affected".

(The reporter from the Bristol Mercury who was covering the trial told his readers that "The Court was then cleared. It had not been so crowded, throughout the whole of the Court Martial, particularly with ladies.")

*

The next day, a Saturday, a Coroner's Inquest was held at the colonel's house. The "very respectable" jury were sworn in and immediately went to view the body of the deceased. The Proceedings of the Inquest recorded that "A more harrowing spectacle could hardly be conceived. The body was lying extended at full length on the outside of the bed, with the head upon the pillow and the mouth and eyes open. The right arm was stretched close by the side and the left, the one with which it is supposed the fatal act was committed, was in a raised position, bending backwards towards the shoulder. The pistol was on the floor, close to the bed. The body was partly undressed, the coat, waistcoat, stock and boots having been taken off. Viewed from the side, with the exception of the ghastly appearance of the countenance, the body was that of a person reposing. On the left, the sight was most distressing. The shirt immediately above the wound was scorched, the breast was encrusted with gore and the channel in which the blood flowed extended to the middle of the bed. Every one present seemed impressed with feelings of pity and regret."

Mrs Ann Pitchforth, the first witness, said she had been housekeeper to the deceased for about sixteen years. The last time she saw him alive was at two o'clock on Friday morning. He had returned home at about eleven but did not retire to his bedroom for some hours. She had heard him walking about for some time. She was once or twice in and out of the sitting-room and saw him with pen, ink and paper. He was throwing papers into the fire. It had always been his custom to kiss and say goodnight to his children ere going to bed, but he did not do so that night, a thing which he had never omitted to do before. . . . She had been that night with the children in the nursery. The deceased went to his room at about two o'clock and about fifteen minutes later she heard a pistol fired there. Being much frightened she waited for a few moments and then going into the bedroom found the deceased lying there.

She had latterly remarked a great difference in the manner of the deceased to what it had been, more marked these last days than before. The deceased used to call her several times for things to be placed before him. He appeared to be a great deal worse since the Court Martial began, especially the first day, when he returned home much distracted. Before that his spirits had been low, and she had remarked that depression ever since the riots. For the last few days he was in the habit of walking about the room and knocking the things about. He would ring the bell and when she came would speak to her as if he was out of his mind. He would then tell her that he did not know what he had said. His state of mind had gradually got worse since Monday last. There was no-one in the room when the occurrence took place. (This witness was in tears while giving her evidence and on retiring from the room she fainted.)

James Wilson, the footman, said he had been in the service of Colonel Brereton for seven years. He saw him for the last time when he came home with his gardener at eleven o'clock on the Thursday night. He held his head down, as if he was in trouble, and did not give his usual commands but entered the house without speaking to him, where he had always been accustomed to speak to him before. He never saw his master afterwards until he was dead. (Here the witness burst into tears.)

Wilson had retired to bed a little after 1 o'clock. He slept in the kitchen along with the gardener. About 3 o'clock in the morning the housekeeper woke him and told him what had happened. He immediately went up to his master's bedroom. The candle was burning on the mantelpiece and there was smoke in the room. On looking into the bed, the curtains of which were drawn, he saw his master quite dead. On going round the side of the bed he perceived a wound and when the shutters were opened the next morning found the pistol that had been discharged lying on the floor near the bedside. . . .

His master had placed his watch, comb and spectacles on the mantelpiece, instead of putting them by his bedside, which was his usual custom. He always had his gun and pistols loaded with balls and slugs in the room, and usually kept his pistols on the chair by the bedside. He was always prepared against robbers, of whom there was much talk in the neighbourhood, which was a remarkably bad one.

Dr Augustus Loinsworth, a physician and surgeon to the forces, said he had known Colonel Brereton first about twenty years before when he had been a major in the West India Rangers. During the last thirteen months he had known him intimately, as he had been his commanding officer in the district. He had parted with the colonel at a quarter before eleven at Reeve's Hotel. The colonel shook hands with him and with another friend, Major Ellard, then got into his gig to go home. He had been with Colonel Brereton since five o'clock and had remarked that his manner was very peculiar. Indeed for the last two months, ever since the riots, he had been in a state of extreme agitation, labouring under a great degree of excitement. He had said and done the most inconsistent things, particularly on the Thursday evening, when he had given the most inconsistent directions to his counsel, Mr Erle, wanting him to propose such things to the Court as a military man, or indeed any man in his senses, must have known would not be acceded to. Indeed so altered was his manner on that occasion that he thought when he parted from him that something unpleasant would happen before morning.

Questioned by a juror: If that was your impression, why did he not prevent the colonel from being alone? — Because, being aware of the great attachment Colonel Brereton bore for his children, it was his impression that he would not do anything against himself while they were in the house. And such was the state of feverish excitement under which the colonel laboured that night that the mere mention of not allowing him to be alone would have increased his complaint tenfold. His excitement had been greater than he had ever observed it.

Colonel Brereton's health latterly had not been good, the doctor continued. He suffered from a visceral complaint, a derangement of the secretions of the liver, for which he had attended him, but he had not reported ill as he was still able to attend to his duties. The complaint had been much aggravated by the state of mind the deceased had been in for the last ten weeks. In fact, at the time of the riots Colonel Brereton was suffering from the effects of a recent severe liver attack, and had been very unfit for making active exertions in such a matter. For the last three months he had been in a state of feverish excitement. His pulse was high, his tongue was loaded and he had little or no appetite. His habits were always exceedingly temperate. . . .

He was an exceedingly fond father and indeed, in his general disposition was a most kind, benevolent and humane man. As to his principles of honour, if anything, he had too high a sense of it.

From the position in which the body lay witness would say that death must have been instantaneous; he could not have struggled a moment, as the ball must have passed through the heart.

*

The jury immediately brought in a verdict that Colonel Brereton had died from a pistol wound inflicted on himself while under a temporary derangement.

While the Inquest was being held the two orphan girls, "who were most interesting children", according to the reporter from the Mercury, were to be observed looking through the cottage window, apparently unconscious of the grievous bereavement which they had suffered.

On a leaf of the Bible used for swearing in the jury were recorded details of his marriage, in Marylebone church, to Miss Olivia Moss, and the births of his children: and the entry: "14th January, 1829, 3 o'clock in the morning, my beloved wife Olivia died at my house at Clifton Wood". As the reporter said, "This obituary drew the attention of some of those present to the remarkable coincidence that they were enquiring into his death on the very anniversary of hers. It was remarked that it was probable, in the abberation of his mind, that he had mistaken the day of the month on which he committed the fatal act."

*

One of the letters written by Tom Brereton during the hours when he alternately paced about or scratched at parchment with a quill was addressed to his uncle, Lieutenant-Colonel Andrew Coghlan, late of the 45th of Foot, who lived in Bath. It read:

My ever dearest uncle,

My unfortunate mind is not now in a state to enter into particulars and I can therefore only hope yourself and my dearest aunt will not forsake my innocent and helpless babes who will be but little sensible when they awake tomorrow of the injustice done to their unfortunate father which deprives them forever of his protection. . . . Do not let poor Pitchforth want, she has been a faithful creature to me. I cannot say more. God in heaven bless you both. T.B.

The colonel went on, in a postscript, to list his debts (which were paltry) and ask that his remains should be placed beside poor Olivia's. Because, in his opinion, it was a waste of money, he asked that no expense should be incurred on his funeral that could be avoided.

The letter was later accepted as being his only Will, and on 2nd April his uncle was granted administration of it, and the guardianship of the two girls.

In another letter written that night, a suicide note, Tom Brereton attributed the main cause of his death as being the gross neglect of the Government in sending an inadequate force to the city and causing Major-General Dalbiac to conduct an infamous and cruelly unjust prosecution against him, with the most malignant and heartless perseverance, in order to show the world that eighty dragoons were sufficient to protect the city against countless thousands of an infuriated mob, and without the smallest assistance from the magistrates or the civil authorities.

Brereton said that Charles Pinney, Ebenezer Ludlow, Abraham Hilhouse and others had sworn the most dreadful falsehoods in order to screen themselves and their brother magistrates, and that Cornet Kelson's evidence had been "false in the extreme". He hoped Major-General Dalbiac would "meet his reward for being the chief cause of depriving my innocent and helpless babes of their only protection in this world" and ended by saying that he left the note as some proof of "the cruelly unjust manner" in which he had been used. He wished it to be published to the world at large as the only satisfaction his friends would have for his untimely death. (It never was, until 1979.)

*

A small cortege departed from Redfield House at seven in the morning on the following Thursday, but many hats were doffed and many heads were bowed as the coffin passed, and "a considerable number of the populace" joined the principal mourners as the procession moved through the streets on the long journey up to the crypt of Clifton Parish church, where the colonel was laid to rest beside the remains of his wife.

The Trial of the Young Officers

On the 7th of January 1832, at the New Court in St George's Chapel, with Sir J.B.Bosanquet presiding and the Duke of Beaufort sitting at his right hand, the trial began of Captain John Lewis, charged with killing and slaying Thomas Morris by shooting him with a leaden bullet.

Mr Ball, for the prosecution, said he was sorry the case had been mixed up with party feeling, and asked the jury not to allow any such feeling to have any weight on their minds, and to dismiss from their thoughts everything they had heard or read about the case and bring in an unbiased judgement. The facts were then recited and then the first witness was sworn:

William Watts, a labourer, residing in Temple Street, said he knew Thomas Morris, he was married to his mother. The boy was turned twelve years of age and was about four feet high and had worked since October for the Bristol Pottery. He had kept the boy at home on the Saturday and the Sunday. He had left home at twenty-past seven on the Monday and witness next saw him at the Infirmary at half-past eight. Just before he died his boy had told him there was no row at all but that a man had pulled out something and shot him.

William Booth, a pig butcher, was about five yards from the boy when he heard the report of a pistol. He turned his head and saw the boy fall. He ran up and saw that the ball had entered the boy's stomach. He saw a gentleman run away and a man jump on his back and bring him down. He had a horse pistol. After about three minutes the constables came to his assistance.

John Sambrook, of Cherry Lane, saw some constables driving a man out of the Square. He did not want to go. The constables left him and a gentleman came up and ordered him to go. He touched him on the back and said "Go on". A second man came up and said to the man in the smock frock "Don't thee move for him!" The gentleman said "Go on, you had better go on." The second man put himself in a daring kind of way and said "I'll be damned if he goes for thee." The gentleman then pulled a pistol from his side pocket and it went off immediately. He did not point at any object at all. A boy nearby dropped.

Thomas Harren, of Bedminster, saw a man who wished to go into the square again. Captain Lewis insisted that he should not and pushed him to prevent him. They had words about it. The captain drew his pistol from his side and shot it off without taking any aim. There was no-one there except Captain Lewis and a man lying dead or drunk. After the pistol was fired Captain Lewis ran off and a sailor caught hold of him. Several constables came up. The captain and the man were both on the ground. The constables beat Mr Lewis, thinking he was one of the rioters.

Henry Haines saw a man striking Captain Lewis over the head three or four times. "I asked him what he had shot the boy for and he said he had been insulted and had done it in his own defence." There were several houses on fire in the square but there was no rioting going on at the time of the shot.

William Morgan, House Surgeon at the Infirmary: Morris was brought about half-past eight. He died about five on the afternoon of the next day from a pistol wound. The ball went through the body except the skin. The shape of the wound was circular; the edges were turned inwards. He had extracted the ball but did not know where it was now. Had not observed the least indentation in it. "It must have taken a direction obliquely upwards, either from having bounded on the ground or from striking against a bone, but I think the former most probable. I asked the boy how it occurred; he said it was accidental; that he had been shot by a constable but that it had not been intended for him but for a man that escaped him."

Captain Lewis then addressed the Court in his defence. He explained that he had been sworn in as a special constable in the December of 1830, because serious riots were expected. Colonel Mair from the Home Office had come to the city especially to arrange for the parishes to be organised. All half-pay officers were ordered to act under the direction of the magistrates for the preservation of the peace. In October he had been away in Devonshire and returned to the city on the day Sir Charles Wetherell made his entry. On the Sunday he was on his way to attend Divine Service at the cathedral when he saw a party of the 14th Light Dragoons being attacked by a mob with stones and glass bottles. They fired a volley and he decided not to go to the cathedral and went instead to the Guildhall. During the course of the day he went to the Bridewell, to the New Gaol, to the Bishop's Palace and to Queen Square. At about two in the morning while endeavouring to stop some ruffians from entering the Custom House he was knocked down and trampled upon, and so much injured that he went home. . . .

When he got up the next morning he was told that the posse comitatus had been called out and was asked to go to the Guildhall. From his experience the previous day he felt it was dangerous to face an infuriated, drunken and lawless mob unarmed, and accordingly decided to take his pistols as a means of self-defence. At the Guildhall he asked Alderman Hilhouse if the constables were authorised to carry firearms; the Alderman replied that if they were resisted in the execution of their duties they should defend themselves the best way they could, with arms or anything else they might have about them.

When he got to the square about seven or half-past it was still burning. Men were lying about in all directions, dead and also stupefied with liquor. He assisted a party of constables to drive a body of men out of the square. One of them did not want to go and lingered behind. He spoke to him and said he was sure from his appearance that he had not been in bed during the night and that it was quite time for him to go. He replied "Nor have you been in bed either, that I know damned well. Why don't you go home yourself?" As they reached the corner two men came up and told the man he was a damned fool if he went any further.

"The man demanded to know who I was and I told him him I was a special constable. On raising my arm to keep him off he immediately collared me, and at the same time I received a severe blow on my temple from one of his companions. I felt that my life was in danger and drew one of my pistols. I immediately received a severe blow just above the elbow, which knocked the pistol down. It went off instantly in my hand. . . . I declare I never intentionally or consciously drew the trigger — the blow caused the pistol to discharge. I heard the cry of a boy and saw him sitting about fifteen yards away. He exclaimed that he was shot. . . . I feel an anguish that I cannot describe that an innocent boy, never seen by me, was the victim."

Nineteen persons were then called to give evidence for the defence, among them:

Alderman Hilhouse, who said he had not the least recollection of Captain Lewis asking if he might use his pistols.

John Harwood, the man in charge of the seamen's floating chapel, who said that on the Sunday he tried to get to the square but on the way saw man behaving in a very riotous manner, using many oaths and much abusive language. He thought he was in bad company and he had better go home but just then he saw a tall gentleman asking a man to leave the square. The man said he was doing no harm and the gentleman said he would do no harm by leaving. By that time they had got to the place where the man who used bad language was standing. He caught hold of Captain Lewis with both hands and as the captain drew his pistol from his bosom it went off instantly.

Cross-examined: The boy fell close to me. I did not exclaim What a shame it was to kill a poor innocent boy; I never spoke.

Richard Lowe, a surgeon, said he had been called upon to attend Captain Lewis on the Wednesday evening. He had a severe contusion on the left temple, involving the eye, and there was the mark of a severe blow crossing the right arm obliquely above the elbow.

Several men then gave evidence as to character, saying that John Lewis was generous, open-hearted, kind, charitable and humane. The learned judge then summed up the evidence and told the jury that if they came to the conclusion that the pistol went off by accident that was the end of the case.

The jury almost immediately pronounced a verdict of Not Guilty, which was received with loud clapping of hands, which, however, the judge rose to restrain, saying that such ebullitions were highly improper and could not be allowed. He added that Captain Lewis left the Court without a stain on his character, that he had done his duty and that it reflected great credit on him.

Mr Ball then applied for the expences of the Prosecution but the learned judge said he must consider the matter; there had been two bills preferred, both of which had been ignored by the Grand Jury.

*

On Wednesday, 25th January 1832, at about one o'clock the officers who had sat in judgement on Lieutenant-Colonel Brereton re-assembled in the Merchant's Hall for the purpose of trying Captain William Warrington of the 3rd Dragoon Guards on charges connected with his conduct during the riots. The Captain, who sat at a table on the left of the President, pleaded Not Guilty to all the charges.

The Prosecuting Officer, Major-General Sir Charles Dalbiac, began by saying that evidence given during the Court of Inquiry held the previous November had appeared to reflect in a serious manner upon the conduct of Captain Warrington. He had therefore not been called to give evidence because his replies might implicate him. Captain Warrington had later asked the Adjutant General that his conduct should be investigated, but since another Inquiry would reveal nothing more the General Commanding in Chief had directed that Captain Warrington's case should be referred to a General Court Martial. Twenty witnesses were called, among them:

Troop Sergeant-Major Martin, who had been on duty with Captain Warrington's troop on the 30th and 31st of October and stated that the troop consisted of 33 men and horses. He said that the troop, or detachments of it, had been called out repeatedly in the course of Sunday the 30th to quell the riots. The detachment on duty at the Bishop's Palace had returned to quarters, Leigh's Bazaar, at about nine o'clock. The troop had then turned out again at midnight, had returned to quarters after a short time, and then at four in the morning two-thirds of it had gone to quell a riot in Queen Square. No NCO or man had been sent to look for the officer commanding troops, Lieutenant-Colonel Brereton, between ten-thirty and four-thirty the next morning.

Thomas Kington, a merchant, who, between ten and half-past ten on the Sunday had asked Captain Warrington, who was mounted at Leigh's Horse Bazaar with the greater part if not the whole of his troop, to bring it to Queen Square to quell a riot. The Custom House was on fire. The captain had replied that he should be most happy and willing to go but could not march his troop without the order of Colonel Brereton. When asked where the colonel was to be found the captain had said "I cannot tell," or words to that effect. The captain had undoubtedly shown a willingness to act if he had orders.

Samuel Goldney, a surgeon, at about three o'clock on the morning of Monday the 31st received a letter from the Mayor addressed to Colonel Brereton or the officer commanding his Majesty's troops. He had delivered the letter to Captain Warrington at Leigh's Bazaar between five and ten minutes later. Warrington told him that Colonel Brereton was not there, but he believed he would be back about six in the morning. He expressed his willingness to do everything in his power but said he could not act without a magistrate going every inch of the road with him. There was some conversation about the 14th having been ordered out of Bristol, during which Captain Warrington said it was clear there was a screw loose somewhere, but where he did not know! He said he had about twenty-five efficient men but that their horses were so tired they were scarcely able to carry them. Notwithstanding that, he was willing to turn out immediately if he could get proper orders or the company of any magistrate.

Questioned by Lieutenant-Colonel Keyte, a member of the Court: When the Captain said he could not act without having a magistrate to go every inch of the road with him, did you take any measures to communicate to the Mayor or any magistrate what Captain Warrington had said? No — I did not know where any magistrate was to be found except the Mayor and he had particularly requested me not to mention where he was to be found.

Alderman Camplin went with several others to the Horse Bazaar at four in the morning for the purpose of calling out the troops. He told Captain Warrington that he was a magistrate and that unless troops were instantly sent to Queen Square the whole place would be burned down. The Captain said that his horses and men were all tired and that he had a letter for Colonel Brereton but could not find him anywhere. The Alderman had read the letter and found it was a very proper one, whereupon Captain Warrington said he could not send more than four and twenty men. The witness said "do not talk of sending but go yourself". The captain then said the troops should not go without a magistrate. Alderman Camplin said he would go with them, but the captain then said they could not go until he had seen Colonel Brereton. They went together to No 2, Unity Street, where they found the colonel, after his presence had been denied by two females who looked out of the window.

Questioned by Captain Warrington: When you told me you were a magistrate did I not say "Come along, then?" Answer: To the best of my knowledge you did not.

F.M. Danson, Esq, was with Alderman Camplin. They were shown to a place covered with straw where there were some dragoons lying down. Some horses were standing on the other side. Shortly afterwards Captain Warrington arrived and on being asked by the Alderman to assist in Queen Square expressed great willingness to come. He said "Very well, sir, the troops are ready," and then asked the Alderman if he would go with them. The Alderman hesitated, and the captain said the troops could not go without a magistrate. Witness had a word or two with Mr Camplin, then said "Of course the Alderman will go down as a magistrate to direct the troops". The captain said he could only send twenty-five troops and when the Alderman asked if he would go himself he replied "No, no, I shall not go with you. I shall send an officer". He then asked what the troops were to do when they got to the square and the Alderman told him "Oh, they will ride in amongst the mob and beat them with the flat of their swords". Captain Warrington said his orders were not to fire. They went to find Colonel Brereton to get the orders changed. There were two women there but he heard no denial of Colonel Brereton. He did not even hear Colonel Brereton enquired for.

Lieutenant and Adjutant Francis, of the Recruiting Staff: About eight o'clock on the evening of the Sunday took an order to the officer commanding 3rd Dragoon Guards for him to proceed to the Bishop's Palace. When he asked where Captain Warrington was he was told he was not there.

Cornet Kelson, at about three o'clock took command of a detachment of the 3rd Dragoons to go to the New Gaol on the orders of Captain Warrington, who remained in his quarters and was there when he returned. At about eight o'clock he was ordered by Colonel Brereton to take a detachment to the Bishop's Palace. Captain Warrington was not then in his quarters, and had not been since seven o'clock. The captain had told him he was going to General Pearson's in Clifton to ask his advice, and that if he was wanted witness was to send there for him. When witness returned to quarters at about half-past nine the captain was in his bedroom in Reeve's Hotel, getting into bed. At a quarter before eleven the mob attacked the hotel and the captain took command of the troop. . . .

Some time before five o'clock on the morning of Monday, the 31st he proceeded to Queen Square in command of a detachment, accompanied by Colonel Brereton. Two sides of the square were on fire; the mob was destroying everything. They charged several times down the street at the back of the Mansion House and in and about the square. At about half-past six witness sent a dragoon by the name of Llewellyn with a message to Captain Warrington to bring up his squadron.

Questioned by Captain Warrington: No, he had never known the captain to use the bedroom before. He was not completely undressed when he saw him. He had asked the captain to lie down and had promised to let him know in person if he was required, or to send an orderly for the reserve party.

Sir Charles Dalbiac then closed the case for the Prosecution. The next day, the fifth of the trial, a surgeon told the Court that Major-General Pearson was ill and would not be in a fit state to attend for some days at least. Captain Warrington was asked by the Court whether, under the circumstances, he thought it advisable to proceed with his defence. He said he would, to the point where the evidence of General Pearson would be required. After a short pause, silence was demanded and the captain proceeded to address the court.

He said that he could only act on the express orders of Colonel Brereton unless a written requisition from a magistrate had released him from that duty. He had had many verbal requests during the Sunday evening and felt he was not bound to act on them or to refer them all to his commanding officer, particularly as he believed it was the intention of the rioters to separate his force.

On the Sunday night, at about half-past three o'clock, a letter was brought by two gentlemen addressed to Lieutenant-Colonel Brereton or the officer commanding His Majesty's troops. He had at first refused to break the seal but after being repeatedly urged by them to do so had read the contents. He then pressed them to take back the letter and deliver it to the colonel, but they refused to receive it. In their presence he had told Sergeant Deane to give directions to the half of the troop which was not bridled up to get ready immediately, firmly believing that the gentlemen were going to Colonel Brereton in the Adjutant's quarters to apprise him of the communication from the Mayor. He much regretted not having sent the letter himself by hand of a military orderly.

He did not deny being absent from his place of duty but it was not the result of indifference or a want of vigour. On all former occasions when he had been employed on similar duties the force under his command had invariably been accompanied by a magistrate, but finding the case so different at Bristol he had wished for the advice of some experienced officer. Although a total stranger to Major-General Pearson he told Cornet Kelson that while the city was quiet he was going to Clifton to ask his advice. He had called on Colonel Brereton before he left to make sure he had no orders — he had not — and then went as fast as he could to General Pearson's and returned immediately to quarters. Captain Warrington trusted the Court would not condemn the motive he had for being absent, although he was ready to admit that strictly speaking he had no right to absent himself for a moment.

As to being accused of retiring to bed, Cornet Kelson had proved that he waited for the detachment to return from the Bishop's Palace. The landlady of Reeve's Hotel had observed some ague symptoms upon him and with difficulty prevailed upon him to retire to a bedroom. The waiter, John Corfield, had already told the court that he could not have been wholly undressed from the short time that elapsed between the attack on the house and his appearance in uniform coming down the stairs. The charge, Captain Warrington said, resolved itself into this; that while suffering from a shivering fit in consequence of his clothes having been wetted repeatedly during twenty-four hours he retired to change.

He was also charged with permitting the detachment to proceed to Queen Square under the sole command of Cornet Kelson. Now the fact was that the detachment was not ordered by him to the scene of the riots, they were not there under the sole command of the said Cornet and he did not remain inactive in his quarters. On the contrary, he remained with ten or twelve men as a reserve, on the express orders of Colonel Brereton. As soon as the rest of his men were ordered to charge he was sent for, and lost not a moment in bringing up the remainder of the troop and putting himself at their head. They afterwards frequently charged the mob and greatly contributed to quelling the riots.

Captain Warrington proposed, with the permission of the Court, to call Major Mackworth, Major Beckwith and officers of the 14th Light Dragoons to state their opinion of his conduct; and to put in several testimonials from officers under whose command he had been, and from magistrates in the South-West District who observed his readiness to co-operate with the civil power.

The captain then made a moving plea: "I have trespassed on the time of the Court," he said, "from regard to the gallant regiment to which I belong, and from the recollection that my father and brother are both soldiers and that my grandfather, great-grandfather and almost every male relation and connexion, for centuries past, have held commissions in the British Army."

Letters were then put in from eight persons, all of them speaking in the very highest terms of Captain Warrington, both as an officer and a gentleman. The captain then called sixteen witnesses in his defence, amongst them:

Private William Denny, who heard Colonel Brereton tell Captain Warrington that the troop was not to turn out except on an order from the colonel or on a requisition signed by two of the magistrates.

Cornet Kelson, who saw Captain Warrington reading a letter at about half-past three on the morning of the 31st and heard the captain, or the troop-sergeant-major, say that it was the King's Regulations that a magistrate should accompany any party sent out.

Sergeant Deane, who saw a note delivered to Captain Warrington at about a quarter before four. When the gentlemen brought the note and asked for the commanding officer he thought they meant Captain Warrington and directed them to the stables, where he was among the horses. The captain asked him to get a light for him to read the note. After reading it he told them he was not the commanding officer, and requested them to take it to Colonel Brereton. They said they had been looking for him for three-quarters of an hour. Captain Warrington expressed his willingness to act if he could get a proper order or be accompanied by a magistrate. He ordered that half the horses that were not bridled up should be bridled up, as he expected to have orders to turn out immediately.

"The two gentlemen went in search of the colonel," Sergeant Deane said, "and a short time afterwards Captain Warrington said to me "My God, what a time those gentlemen are away!" Soon after, another gentleman arrived. The captain said he was ready and willing to act at any moment if he could only see a magistrate. The gentleman said "I am a magistrate" and Captain Warrington replied "Then accompany me." The gentleman hesitated for some time and then asked if that was according to regulation, and on being told it was, asked the captain to go along with him to find Colonel Brereton, which they did."

Thomas Darrell went with the captain to Colonel Brereton's lodgings in Unity Street, where he heard the colonel say "I do not know what is to be done, I have no orders".

Thomas Pompett, servant to General Pearson, said that Captain Warrington arrived at Prospect Cottage, Somerset Place, Clifton between six and seven o'clock and stayed for four or five minutes. (At this point, after discussion with the Court, Captain Warrington agreed to withdraw the affidavit sent in evidence by General Pearson as he trusted his motives for absenting himself must be apparent to the Court.)

John Calkin, a waiter at Reeve's Hotel said he was sent for some medicine for the captain on the Sunday evening. Cornet Kelson, recalled, said he had observed that the captain was ill.

Private Denny, who heard Colonel Brereton tell the captain to remain with a few men as a reserve when the troop was called out from Leigh's Bazaar on the morning of the 31st. The captain said "I would much rather go myself" but the colonel replied "No, Captain, I think you are very much fatigued and want some rest, for you look very poorly." The captain said he was not more so than Cornet Kelson and the rest of his troop but Colonel Brereton rode off instantly and desired him to take his advice.

*

On the Sixth day, the 31st of January 1832, the Court heard Major Mackworth say that Captain Warrington did his duty in an active and intelligent manner and that he instantly and effectively obeyed the orders he was given. He showed no want of vigour. Major Beckwith then told the Court that it would be impossible for him to give a correct idea of Captain Warrington's conduct unless he was permitted to give some detail of the circumstances in which he was placed. The President desired the witness to confine himself to what affected the captain, and that only.

Major Beckwith said that he found the Mayor and the magistrates bewildered and stupified with terror. He urged that one or more of them accompany him on horseback for the purpose of restoring order but they all refused to do so. . . . — At this point the President told Major Beckwith to confine himself to what affected the captain. The major replied that his only object was to show the situation in which the captain was placed. The President declared that it was as much his duty to protect other parties from implication as to protect the prisoner. The major nevertheless continued: "they all refused, stating that it would make them unpopular and cause their property to be destroyed. They also said that none of them could ride on horseback. Seeing, therefore, that assistance from them was out of the question I demanded, and obtained, a written authority to take what measures I deemed expedient. "The impression I had," Major Beckwith continued, "was that Captain Warrington was, in a great measure, paralysed by the imbecility and misconduct of those who ought to have directed him. He appeared to me to be alert, zealous and desirous to do his duty, and at no time did he evince a want of vigour and activity."

Questioned by the Court as to whether he alluded to the officer commanding or the magistrates when he used the phrase "ought to have directed him" Major Beckwith replied "To both".

Captain Gage, of the 14th Light Dragoons told the Court that Captain Warrington had shown quite the reverse of a want of vigour and Lieutenant Dawson of the 14th said that he had observed that Captain Warrington was unwell during the time of the riots.

The defence then closed and the Court adjourned for thirty-six hours to enable the Prosecutor to prepare his reply. When the Court re-assembled at eleven o'clock on Thursday, 2nd February 1832 Captain Warrington put in a document signed by the General Officer Commanding South West District directing that no troop was to be taken out for the suppression of riots without the written requisition or the personal attendance of a magistrate.

Sir Charles Dalbiac then addressed the Court at great length. He admitted that the absence of all civil authority during the awful night of Sunday until four or five on the Monday must have proved prejudicial to the small military force then employed in Bristol. Despite that, it did not relieve the prisoner of any material part of the accusation against him. In particular Captain Warrington had pleaded that he could not turn out his troop unless he had specific orders to do so from Colonel

Brereton, but had then done just that when Reeve's Hotel was attacked. Further, the troop-sergeant-major had stated that nobody was sent to look for Colonel Brereton between half-past ten on Sunday night, when the prisoner was aware, from having been told by Mr Kington, that the mob was destroying the Custom House, and half-past four the next morning, a period when the robber and the incendiary were proceeding uncontrolled from atrocity to atrocity.

The Prosecutor went on to say that the prisoner had been in possession of the letter from the Mayor for an hour and ten minutes without acting upon it. About forty minutes had been wasted in various parleys and discussions and in gaining admittance to the place where Colonel Brereton had taken up his residence, whereas if he had acted upon the letter as soon as he broke the seal the troop would have got to Queen Square at about half-past three instead of at five o'clock. The south-west wing of the west side of Queen Square could have been saved. The letter had been put in the prisoner's pocket with almost as much indifference as if it had been an invitation to dinner. By neglecting to act on it he had compromised not only himself but his superior in command and the honour of His Majesty's arms.

It appears that Captain Warrington was absent for a period of about two hours: "I have nothing further to add," General Dalbiac said, "the charge is proved. It is extraordinary that when the prisoner returned to find only five men of his troop and horses left in the Bazaar, and being aware of the appalling state of the city and observing the conflagrations then vomitting forth in various parts of it, he showed no anxiety or even curiosity to enquire what his troop was doing or whether his own services could be of any avail. I do not doubt that he felt unwell, but he was capable of walking to Clifton and back and taking command of the troop outside the hotel.

No illness, short of absolute destruction of health, should have restrained the prisoner from searching for his men."

General Dalbiac continued: "Captain Warrington has several times spoken of the orders issued during the disturbances which occurred in the winter of 1830–31. I can speak well of those instructions because they were the same as those issued by me to every officer and non-commissioned officer of cavalry in Kent, Sussex and Surrey, where I held the command of troops sent into the district to put down the disturbances. These orders are well known to three members of this Court, who then commanded regiments under my orders. But surely those orders do not apply to an officer placed in command of a troop under circumstances during which rioters were systematically progressing from outrage to outrage without check. Does the prisoner mean to infer that if Winchester Gaol had been forced by a body of rioters he would have ignored them unless a magistrate were present? On this subject the Lord Chief Justice of the Common Pleas had the following to say: 'It is mistaken to think that because men are soldiers they cease to be citizens; they are as much bound to prevent a breach of the peace as any other citizen. In 1780 this mistake extended to an alarming degree; soldiers with arms in their hands stood by and saw houses pulled down by persons whom they might lawfully have put to death but they did not prevent them because they had no officer to give them a command or because there was no Justice of the Peace with them. It is the duty of soldiers to prevent a crime being committed.' To come to our own immediate time, the Lord Chief Justice, at the opening of the Special Commission in this city three weeks ago, said that by the common law every person may lawfully endeavour, by his own authority, to suppress a riot by every means in his power, and he may be assured that he will be supported and justified by the common law.

"I do not advocate that British troops, in the absence of a peace officer are to take redress into their own hands on every trifling tumult or disturbance but I do boldly affirm that the first public service due from the soldier is the maintenance of the law which preserves a man's person from death and his property from injury. Are our services to be used only against a foreign enemy? Do we have no domestic service to perform? Shall the rebel, the robber and the incendiary stalk forth in our streets and His Majesty's troops be told they can lay no hand on them but in the presence of a magistrate? Shall our gaols be forced and the felons be loosed upon society? Shall the aged and infirm, the nursing mother and the nestling infant be torn from their beds at the dead of night and British troops be taught to stand by and look on? God forbid! I say, God in Heaven forbid!

"I now commit the prisoner into the hands of this honourable Court and I pray that his trial may be productive of benefits, not merely to the interests of the British Army but to the interests of the nation at large. And may the flames of Bristol serve as a beacon to every town and city in the United Kingdom!"

After asking Captain Warrington if he had anything further to offer in his defence the President cleared the Court and the members continued in consultation for several hours.

*

Although the Court unanimously and most earnestly submitted to the Judge Advocate General that there were strong extenuating circumstances — lack of experience, errors of judgement rather than lack of a sense of duty, the very favourable testimony of many witnesses — the captain was found guilty on all counts except one;

(that relating to him allowing the detachment to proceed to Queen Square while he remained inactive in quarters) and was sentenced to be cashiered. That decision was confirmed by the King, but he extended "his most gracious clemency" to the young officer by allowing him to sell his commission.

William Henry Warrington retired from the army in mid-March and soon after that Cornet Kelson purchased the rank of lieutenant in the same regiment, indirectly because of the vacancy created by the departure of the unfortunate captain, he of the long military antecedents. But whatever his shortcomings he was too much of a gentleman ever to disclose the advice he was given by Major-General Pearson on that fateful night when he dragged himself up the hill to Clifton in the pouring rain, only to be thrown out four minutes later. It seems probable that the only communication was a short, sharp, military expletive advising him to perform an impossible function.

*

The Felons

Felony: "A grave crime punishable by penal servitude or death".

His Majesty's Commission for the trial of the Bristol rioters began on Monday, the 2nd of January 1832. In the course of the preceding week the Sheriffs had sworn-in nearly all householders in the city as special constables, more than two thousand of them, under "an organised system of subordination". In addition to the sizeable force thus created a body of men were also formed for the protection of the Judges. These, under the control of Mr Dowling, were dressed in a uniform similar to that worn by the Metropolitan Police, while the specials were identified by the name of their parish or district, printed on calico or card and placed in their hatband or pinned to their jacket.

At an early hour these expectant and suddenly important people assembled at their churches, then made their way to the Exchange, where they were assigned to their duties: columns of men slowly converged down the spokes of the wheel on the city centre and then tramped out again en masse on the Bath road.

By ten o'clock the streets to Temple Gate and the road beyond it to Totterdown were lined with constables, while in the city detachments of soldiers were held in readiness in case they should be needed: some of the 52nd of Foot in front of the Wool Hall, more infantry in the Merchant Tailor's Hall in Broad Street, 7th Fusiliers and 75th of Foot at the New Gaol and the 14th Light Dragoons at the Riding-School in Portwall Lane. The Wool Hall, the Tailor's Hall and the Armoury in Stapleton Road had been fitted up as barracks.

At half-past ten the Judges' coaches, each drawn by four greys, were seen approaching from Bath. Amid a flourish of trumpets the lawmen were handed into the carriages provided for their reception and, "with not a single indication of disrespect being apparent", made their way into the city, to 6, Park Street, where they donned their robes of office. Then, in state, led by the City Swordbearer wearing his fur hat — Ye Cappe of Maintenance — and carrying the unharmed Great Sword (made about 1450 and still regularly carried before the Lord Mayor of Bristol), preceded by the Mayor and followed, draggle-tailed, by the Corporation, they solemnly processed to the cathedral to hear Divine Service conducted by the Reverend J. Cross, assisted by a full choir. The preacher, the Reverend Professor Lee, chose as his theme "The Throne is established in Righteousness", and told them that "while Weeping might endure for a night, Joy cometh in the morning". After a light luncheon the Judges made their way to the Guildhall, where there was only an urchin and a ragamuffin or two present to see the elderly Duke of Beaufort, the Lord Lieutenant of Gloucestershire, greet them. They bowed back, sorted themselves into order of precedence and walked, holding their nosegays, into the hall, where, at two o'clock they began the business of the trials.

The Royal Commission was proclaimed and the list of cases read out, then twenty-four members of a Grand Jury, from whom the twelve good-men-and-true would be chosen for each trial, were sworn in. After the usual proclamation against vice and immorality had been read the Lord Chief Justice addressed the court, stressing that it was the duty of every citizen to suppress a riot, one of the most dangerous acts in defiance of the law — the first object of which was to give freedom to men's persons and the second of which was to ensure the safety of their property.

*

The first case to be heard was that of six men, including William Clarke, a strong, muscular young fellow, who were arraigned for destroying the New Gaol, to which they all pleaded Not Guilty. Clarke, whose mother kept the Hen and Chicken Inn at Bedminster, worked in a timber-yard. Calling himself Thomas and saying he was looking for his brother William, he had been apprehended outside a public house in Liverpool on the 5th of November, a very smart piece of work by his parish constable.

Twenty-three people gave evidence against Clarke, saying they had seen him, wearing a light fustian (corduroy) jacket, at the Bridewell and the Cut, at one time carrying a five foot long iron crow-bar across his shoulder, at another with stolen books in his hands and at yet another with bottles in his arms — and even at one time eating a lump of bacon which he said had belonged to Billy Humphries, the Governor of the New Gaol. Clarke was alleged to have made remarks such as "Hurrah! now, me boys!", "Come on, comrades", "We'll have liberty", "Come on there, look sharp!" and, according to Harriet Vowles, a barmaid at the Britannia tavern in All Saints' Street: "Look here, you bastards!"

157

when urging the mob to follow him. In the Boar's Head public house he had flourished a large bunch of keys, saying "Here are the keys of Lawford's Gate prison, and this is the daddy of them all, which will open every jail in England! There will not be one left standing in a fortnight." At one time Clarke had boasted that he had broken open three prisons; that he had done a good day's work that day but hoped he would do a better one the next. . . ..

One man, J.E. Carver, who had been in the debtor's wing of the New Gaol at the time of the riots, aware of the dire implications of giving evidence on a capital charge, chickened out and said he had been extremely ill, had lost his memory and could scarcely recollect any of the circumstances connected with the riots. Nevertheless, dithering, he said he thought he had seen Clarke at the New Gaol but could not say positively that he had been there though the last memory he had was of seeing Clarke strike at the gates with a sledgehammer. . . ..

James Cross, a merchant, had seen Clarke in the Horse and Jockey. In his opinion he had acted like a madman, while R.H. Trickey said Clarke was "overtaken in drink". William Lowe and several others said that Clarke appeared to be deranged, but that a little liquor had a stranger effect on him than on most men, a point that was made much of by the defence. A butcher, James Stokes, said Clarke had purchased a bullock's heart from him on the morning of the 30th; he had known him from childhood; several years back Clarke had received serious injuries when he was hit on the head by a piece of falling timber, a scene that was graphically painted for the court by a sawyer who had been working with him at the time: the unfortunate lad's head had been jammed between two balks of wood and he had hung by it.

When young Clarke saw his mother arrive in the witness box to defend him he fainted. After she had explained how he had been at home until she left for church, and that her son had at times appeared to be foolish ever since the accident, the prisoner was helped out of the court. He returned soon after but again fainted, and a chair had to be provided for him to sit on. Resuming her evidence Mrs Clarke said that on one occasion her son had threatened to kill his nephew, but had then added "Why should I kill him? He has never done me any harm". He knew, on the following morning, that he was not right, she said.

Eighteen men gave evidence of good character on Clarke's behalf, several of them saying that he was very peaceable when he was sober but apt to be outrageous and "rather flighty" when in drink. One, John Pickering, swore that he and Clarke and two other young men went to the Britannia tavern at about two o'clock on the afternoon of the 30th where they had a half pint of gin and then, between them, consumed three-and-a-half gallons of beer, about seven pints apiece — although Clarke drank more than his share. (Presumably they shared the gin as "nips", chasing it down with beer.) Pickering had collected the money to pay for the beer amongst them and it ran out at around sixpence each. Someone else had paid for the gin. (The price of beer has not kept pace with inflation despite the fact that in the last 150 years successive governments have taxed it heavily. If it had it would now be about 110 pence a pint.) Clarke, he said, seemed a little the worse for drink when they left at about a quarter-past three. . . .

The evidence against the other five persons, even that sworn against Patrick Kearney, who was an Irish itinerant vendor of linen drapery, was superficial and unsubstantiated. For example, a lad of ten, William Daven, said a man very much like Patrick Kearney had asked him to fetch some straw for him and when he had done so poured some Turps on it and set fire to it but he was not quite sure that Kearney was the man. If not, he was very much like him. . . . Amongst others, Nancy Carrow, Elizabeth Grant and Nancy Day spoke up on behalf of the accused.

Summing up for three hours, the Lord Chief Justice told the jury that it was their duty to give the accused the benefit of the doubt should the balance of probability hang evenly, a rather unfortunate choice of phrase in the circumstances. While the Judge was speaking Clarke fainted again and water was obtained for him. As he showed no signs of recovery he was then taken away from the bar, the Judge asking if there was a medical man in attendance. There was not, but after a few minutes Clarke pulled himself together and returned. A glass of brandy was procured, he drank it and was allowed to sit on a chair while the Judge concluded his summing-up.

When the jury returned after three hours absence they found Clarke and four others guilty, and one man not guilty. One of those found guilty, Higgs, had called four witnesses as to character: two did not appear but one who did swore Higgs had been at home at the time when he was alleged to have been setting fire to the jail. However, the jury clearly preferred to believe Charles Cressy, who had said he saw Higgs at the New Gaol picking pockets and destroying the gates of the prison.

During the evidence it had been said that a great many Irish people had been seen dragging away loot from the prisons. The keys of the jails which Clarke had proudly shown to anyone who would look had, it seems, gone astray.

*

On the third day, having tried two men on another,

less serious, charge — the burning of the Bishop's Palace — on the fourth another jury was called to hear the evidence against Clarke, Kearney and three other men who were charged with pulling down, destroying and setting fire to the Bridewell and the house belonging to Thomas Evans the Governor. The prisoners pleaded Not Guilty.

Having heard Tom Evans' evidence Clarke once again fainted but this time a surgeon, Mr Shorland, was in attendance and he soon recovered. Evans had said he was unable to identify any of the persons concerned in the riots but Stone the Turnkey identified three of the prisoners as having been there, including Kearney, who, he said, had been standing around with his hands in his pockets. As before, several people, including the chief constable of Bedminster, spoke up for Clarke, saying that he was an honest and peaceable fellow. One, Benjamin Flook, said he had been with Clarke in the Britannia tavern. He had wanted to go home for his dinner but had not done so until he had eventually asked the time and been told it was half-past three, when he had decided he really must go as he usually dined at two o'clock on a Sunday. He did not know the name of the man who had paid for the half pint of gin.

In his summing-up the learned Judge, referring to Clarke's defence of temporary derangement due to excessive liquor, said that dreadful indeed would be the state of society if such a plea were allowed to operate for, conscious of his infirmity, his duty was to abstain altogether; to keep out of temptation.

After less than five minutes' retirement the jury returned to the court and brought in a verdict of guilty. Kearney, when he heard it said "It isn't fair, I be damned if it is!") The court then adjourned, at half-past eight o'clock.

*

The next day, the 6th of January, fifteen prisoners were charged with setting fire to or destroying houses, amongst them Thomas Gregory and Richard Vines. One, Michael Sullivan, pleaded guilty to his charge, saying he had been drunk and fighting all night but had not set fire to anything. (He was later sentenced to be transported for life.)

Evidence was given that Gregory had entered Mr Strong's house and thrown papers, boxes and things of every description into the street from an upstairs window, and on coming out had two candlesticks in his pocket and "unknown things hidden in his bosom". When he saw a man carrying a table from Mr Strong's house he asked if it was a Reform table, and when he was told it was let the man pass. (It was remarked that women were very active in carrying away property.) Soon after, Gregory again entered the house with a group of men who were carrying a torch made of rolls of paper. The house quickly went up in flames, which came out through the tiles.

After a short absence the jury found Gregory guilty.

*

In the case of Richard Vines, evidence was given that he set fire to the house of the Reverend Charles Buck, on the West side of Queen Square. He was seen lighting a fire with paper and feeding the flames with furniture. An onlooker had addressed him with the words "So, Richard, you are busy," to which he had replied, "with the most perfect coolness and not ashamed of his actions," "To be sure, I am".

John Scott, who lived in Shirehampton, five miles away, said there was such a blaze that not six people remained in bed there. He and five others had walked into town to see what was happening. He knew the prisoner by his voice and his face. (At this Vines told the witness that "It's an odd thing to swear to a man by his voice".) The Judge then told Vines that if he had any questions he might put them to the witness or he, the Judge, would do it for him. Vines replied "If it please you, My Lord, anything your Lordship may think proper", but, as it turned out, had nothing further to ask. One of the Shirehampton visitors, R. Gilbert, said he saw Vines, wearing a smock-frock and a cap with flaps over his ears, feeding the flames in a house in the square. (At this point Vines produced a "Scotchman's" cap out of his pocket and said "That's the cap I always wear!") When Gilbert said "The room was on fire when I saw you in it" Vines turned to the Judge and said "I have nothing more, my Lord, to say to that man," and then, addressing the witness, said indignantly "You've swored — the Lord have mercy on your poor soul."

A sailor, William Boon, said that he went to the square for the same reason as a lot of people, out of curiosity. He saw Vines try to break open a door. He could not do it by himself and said "damn your eyes, come on!" whereupon some men went to assist him and broke the door down. When he asked Vines to leave off he answered "It be no business of yours, therefore mind thy business and I'll mind mine."

Vines said he had been in bed all night and had witnesses to prove it. However, none appeared to speak for him when they were called and after a short adjournment the jury found him guilty.

*

On the sixth day one Timothy Collings was indicted for setting fire to Charles Pinney's stable at the Mansion House. According to the contemporary account of the trials the prisoner's appearance was most wretched. He was a native of Ireland and spoke with a strong Irish accent and seemed so stupid as scarcely to understand the nature of the proceedings. . . .

In evidence, a constable said he saw the prisoner take up a fire brand and then drop it because it was too hot to hold. He saw two men enter the stable with a firebrand but could not be sure it was the same firebrand or that the prisoner was one of the two. About five minutes after he saw smoke issue therefrom. Two days later he apprehended the prisoner on Durdham Down and on examining his hands found one of them to be burnt. When asked how it had happened the prisoner told him it had been burnt with a spade. Martha Phillips too had seen someone set fire to the stable but like the constable she could not swear it was the prisoner at the bar.

When Collings was told that if he had anything to say to the jury now was the time to say it he called upon the Lord Jesus Christ and said "He knows that I am not guilty no more than the child who was born only last night". After a few moments consultation the jury asked for the constable to be recalled since they wished to ask him if he was quite sure the prisoner was the man who first carried the firebrand. When asked, Constable Ford said he had not the slightest doubt. After again conferring for a few minutes the jury found the prisoner guilty, but made a recommendation to mercy.

Timothy Collings was also transported for life.

*

On the Seventh day Joseph Kayes, a gentleman's coachman, was indicted for destroying the house belonging to Charles Bull. The owner's son said he had seen the prisoner in the courtyard with several other men. Another witness said he had seen Kayes in the house and shortly afterwards, in about three minutes, the place was completely ablaze. The prisoner had been wearing a light corduroy coat over a black-and-yellow striped waistcoat. (Here Kayes, who was still wearing the same clothes, buttoned up his coat.) Sarah Weeks, a servant girl, said that Kayes said "Damn your heart, if you go in I'll kill you," when she tried to enter a neighbouring house while Martha Davis, another servant (who was awarded £10 by the Judge for her extraordinary courage in defying the rioters) said Kayes had pushed her and told her to stand aside.

At the conclusion of the trial the prisoner addressed the jury in a strong Irish accent, saying it was all a spite and a grudge by Mr Bull, who had brought people to swear against him. He was innocent of all the charges, and that was the God's truth. He then burst into tears and ran down the steps of the dock into the cell below, from where he was dragged up again. Not long after the jury returned and the foreman announced that they found Kayes guilty.

*

On the ninth day Christopher Davis was arraigned on ten counts of having riotously and tumultuously destroyed the New Gaol. Opening the case, the Attorney General said Davis filled a respectable situation in life. He was a man of family, well known, and one from whom better things might have been expected. "We shall find him," he said, "in so many places, and at such short intervals of time, that he will almost appear to have the ability to be in several places at once". Davis had boasted, he went on, of having partaken of the repast provided in the Mansion House for the Recorder, duck and roast beef etcetera, "using some such foolish expression as 'What a shame it is that there should be so much waste when there are so many poor wretches starving'".

Davis had been apprehended, by an accountant who was after the reward, in a house in Sutton Montis, hiding between the joists of an unfloored attic. He said he had left Bristol on the advice of his friends but that he was happier now that he had been found than he had been for some time. On his way back to Bristol he had remarked "There is one thing against me, it is something that I said," but had declined to say what it was.

Nineteen witnesses gave evidence against Davis who at the time of the offences was looking very respectable, wearing a black coat, drab kerseymere breeches and top boots and carrying an umbrella and a stick. Amongst the many things he said, in the midst of all the bustle, cheering and confusion, from time to time putting his hat on his umbrella and waving it about, were "Damn and blast the Bishops and the Corporation", "This is the end of your bloody bishops and magistrates — we'll send them all to hell, damned robbers that they are", "Down with all these churches and mend the roads with them", "Hurrah, go it, my boys!", "Now, damn, won't we have Reform? This is what ought to have been done years ago". On his way to the Bridewell, swinging his umbrella, he had called out "Damn their eyes, burn them, down with them". On the Sunday, he had said to a toll-gate keeper: "Where now is your damned Corporation and your damned Dock Company?!" and in reply to an Irishman who said "Mr Davis, this is the blaze of liberty!," "I wish I had had a hundred men such as you with me last night". To Richard James, a carver and gilder, he had said, catching hold of his hand, "I'm damned, James, this is glorious. This is the sort of thing we want" and: "If they don't take care every bloody church in England will be down before long". Outside the Bishop's Palace he had told William Harvey, a printer, that the bishops were the cause of all this; that it was a shame that one bishop could have £40,000 a year when so many poor people were starving. Later, in a public house, he had advised people to fornicate with the bishops, the churches and the magistrates.

On the Monday, no doubt with the consequences of his actions beginning to dawn on him, Davis had told someone that the events of the past two days had been dreadful, and that he hoped "they" would all be punished for it. (The Court decided that evidence of what he said after the time referred to in the charges was not admissible.)

Davis it was who had been present at the dedication of the church at Bedminster and had called out about bishops being paid £40,000 a year, and he it was who had given money to the poor wretches who ran away from the New Gaol naked. Several people spoke up on his behalf, saying he was an honest, upright, industrious, benevolent and peaceable man, and even some of those who gave evidence against him added before they left the witness box that he was a good fellow. Nevertheless, after an absence of an hour-and-a-half, the jury brought in a verdict of guilty.

The verdict, it was reported in the local newspapers, appeared to create a general surprise.

*

On Thursday, the 12th of January, the prisoners who had been convicted of a capital offence were brought up to receive sentence. First, Christopher Davis, Joseph Kayes, Richard Vines, Thomas Gregory and William Clarke were placed at the bar.

After the judges had donned their black caps, the prisoners were in turn asked if they had anything to say regarding why sentence of death should not be passed. When it came to Kayes' turn he fell down in a fit of agony and his convulsed frame had to be restrained by six men. Writhing around he shouted "Oh, I'm not guilty! I'm not guilty. Oh, my God! My wife, my children!" By order of the Lord Chief Justice he was taken back to the cell below but for a considerable time his ravings could be heard in the court and created a great sensation. Several females fainted and were carried out. Gregory turned to address the court in broken sentences, saying "Oh, my dear Lord, I am innocent; as innocent as a child unborn. Oh, have mercy on me, my dear Lord!" Vines repeatedly implored mercy and Clarke leaned his head over the rail, apparently exhausted. Only Davis retained his composure — for the time being.

The Lord Chief Justice told them that it was impossible to say what their motives had been; it was not the pressure of want or misery and there was no grievance, imagined or real, under which they laboured. They were a striking and awful example of the wickedness which men commit. After admonishing each of them in turn, except Kayes, who was still shrieking down below, he pronounced the last sentence of the law: "That you, and every one of you, be taken hence to the place from whence you came and from thence to a place of execution, where you be severally hanged by the neck until you are dead. And may the Lord, in His infinite goodness, have mercy on your guilty souls". Realising at last the full enormity of what he had just heard Davis wrung his hands and exclaimed "Oh, my Lord, I hope you will have mercy. I never meddled with anything, I never meddled with fires. I was never in a jail before. I hope, my Lord, you will have mercy on me."

He and the others were then taken away and nineteen lesser offenders were brought before the court. Each in turn was sentenced to death but then the Judge told them that he would make a humble recommendation to His Majesty that their lives should be spared. However, "they would not get away lightly; they would spend the rest of their lives in a foreign and distant land, separated for ever from parents, relations and friends, in a state of severe labour and constant privation". Kearney then exclaimed "I'm deprived of my liberty owing to false swearing but I don't care, my life is spared. Ireland is free. Little Ireland for ever!" and did a little jig.

After the Lord Chief Justice had left the city for London Kayes was brought before Mr Justice Bosanquet, who pronounced sentence of death on him. Kayes left the court loudly protesting that he had been wrongfully judged and was a murdered man.

*

On Friday the 27th of January, fifteen days after sentence had been passed and despite a petition to the King signed by ten thousand Bristolians, "including several merchants of the greatest respectability", Davis, Clarke, Gregory and Kayes were hanged over the entrance to the ruined New Gaol. Only the day before Vines, the youngest of the five, had been told that his sentence had been commuted to perpetual banishment, on the grounds that he was an idiot, and that he was to be sent to Australia.

As the end of their lives approached the four condemned men became more and more resigned to the inevitable. The prison chaplain, the Reverend William Day, assisted by his son, gave them daily spiritual consultation, augmented now and then by the voice of the Reverend Thomas Roberts. On the Thursday their wives, the children of Kayes and Gregory, and other relations and friends came to say farewell. Clarke, who was unmarried, told a near relative that he would rather be hanged than transported for life.

Before daybreak on the Friday the clergymen joined the prisoners and shortly after nine o'clock two members of the Press were admitted to the jail. At ten, the four men were given breakfast and soon after a detachment of the 75th of Foot were paraded in front of the ruins of the Governor's house. At eleven, the Sheriffs were met by an honour guard of soldiers drawn from the 7th Fusiliers, at which time the men were taken to the condemned room, where the irons were struck off their feet and their hands were bound. Reading the scriptures, praying, and frequently asking the priests to warn people of the sin of Sabbath-breaking and drunkenness, to which they attributed their dreadful plight, the men passed their last moments on earth. All of them seemed to be tranquil.

In order to preserve the peace of the city, similar measures had been taken as for the arrival of the Judges, except that a number of tradesmen took to their horses and acted as a mounted patrol and the posse comitatus was even bigger than before. By far the greatest number of spectators, some thousands of them — but fewer than when the jail was attacked — subdued, still and silent, had taken up their positions on the opposite side of the Cut, waiting in a bitterly cold wind for the appointed hour of noon. However, it was after one o'clock before the prisoners were led out — preceded by the Reverend Day reading the burial service — whereupon there was a great sigh of sympathy. People murmured such things as "There's Davis, unfortunate fellow," "The Lord receive their souls", and "God save us, there's the poor lad Clarke". A great number of them, including many of the special constables, started to weep.

On the scaffold Gregory was placed on the left, then Davis, then Kayes then Clarke. Ropes were put around their necks and a white hood was placed on their foreheads. They then embraced each other and kissed each others hands, the hands of the Divines who attended them and the hand of Governor Humphries, who also shed tears. With each of them expressing a strong belief in the hope of eternal happiness Gregory stood like a soldier on parade and the others remained still. (The previous April Davis had attended the execution of a man found guilty of burglary and when it was over had turned to the friend who was with him and exclaimed "It is horrible! God only knows who will be next".) Clarke, when his turn came to have the hood drawn down over his eyes, begged for a moment of time and then bowed three times to the crowd.

Each in turn then forgave the executioner, who was a poor, dirty, ragged and wretched-looking person who had taken the job as a desperate means of earning a few pennies. While he was fixing the ropes around their necks he shook so violently that to prevent him from falling off the scaffold one of the jailers had to hold him but, clawing at the shoulders of Kayes and Gregory to steady himself, he eventually completed the task and with a trembling hand pulled the lever.

In the middle of their prayers the four voices of the condemned men were suddenly cut off by the jarring crash of the platform as it gave way under their feet. They plunged down and then their bodies hung, swinging gently from side to side, like grim exclamation marks, in front of the silent, bare-headed and aghast crowd. Except for Kayes, who twitched and writhed for several minutes.

*

171

Epilogue

For some days after the rioting in Bristol there were civil disturbances in Worcester, Coventry, Nottingham, Leeds and other places. The nation, despite the opinion of the Lord Chief Justice, had real cause for grievance and the events of late 1831, in particular Bristol's part in them, did much to spur a sudden and sharp awareness of the need for a change of attitudes by the people who governed the country — a realisation that they must defer to the majority and show greater compassion for their fellow creatures.

In 1835 the Tolpuddle martyrs of Dorset were transported for obstinately demanding the right to act collectively to secure better wages; their actions, together with the deep-rooted feelings of unrest which remained in the population, were part of the movement which brought about change. Democracy, weak though it may have been, and a shadow of what it should have been, brought about Reform in the United Kingdom and, in 1835, thirty years or so before the United States, the abolition of slavery in the British Empire.

Soon after the riots a local commission was elected by Bristol ratepayers to negotiate compensation for the loss and damage incurred during the two hectic days of pillage and arson. 121 actions involving claims for £150,000 (about £6·5m today) were instigated by the losers but when the proceedings ended four years later the settlements made cut the amount paid by the city almost to a third of that. The Bishop had asked for £10,000 for the loss of his Palace but when the matter was referred to Bridgwater assizes he was awarded £6,000. (By abandoning most of their own claims for compensation the magistrates tacitly admitted responsibility for not having taken proper control during the riots, and indeed some of them contributed £500 towards the losses sustained by individuals.)

A report on Bristol's Corporation published in the same year, 1835 (during which the city got its first permanent police force) said that it was "constituted on the closest principles of self-selection and irresponsibility and was a very unfavourable specimen of the results of such a system". There was no evidence that the Aldermen and Councillors had appropriated revenues but they had shown a desire for power, had disregarded complaints, and fenced the Corporation around with privileges; and were guilty of mismanagement, of extravagance, of maintaining an overgrown establishment and of displaying "state magnificence". Over the years they had been careless of the interests of the port and had actually done things which were damaging to it.

Though the men transported to the other end of the earth had been as good as written off by their loved ones one of them, crafty fellow that he was, managed to return and went to the Council House to see the silver platter he had stolen, commenting that whoever had mended it had made a good job of it! Ives, who had been accused of conspiring to take over the ship on the way to

Australia, was one of the handful who ever came back. Most died, sooner or later, though some left a token of their existence behind in the shape of offspring whose descendants are living today. Vines, the lad who only just escaped the gallows on that cold January afternoon, absconded from the farm on which he worked and as a punishment was given hard labour on a road-making team. After more escapes he was put in a chain-gang and then, for further offences, was sentenced to 75 lashes. On 31st December 1839, still not thirty, he died while working on the roads of Hobart, Tasmania, a long, long way from home.

When the provisions of the Reform Act were put into effect the constituency of Boroughbridge was disbanded and Sir Charles Wetherell lost his seat in Parliament. However he remained the Recorder of Bristol and in 1839 a statue was erected in his honour in Clifton. He died in 1846, aged 77, as a result of injuries received in a carriage accident. Daniel Burges the Mayor's secretary became the Town Clerk when Ebenezer Ludlow was appointed chairman of Gloucestershire Quarter Sessions, an appointment he held from 1842 to 1849. He died, aged 75, in 1852. Colonel Digby Mackworth also died in that same year aged 63. Though he tried but failed to get into House of Commons during the 1840s, he was the Sheriff of Monmouthshire in 1843. William Beckwith, despite his honesty and forthright evidence during the trials, became a general, and died a venerable and much respected man in 1871, aged 74, having been High Sheriff of Durham in 1858 and Regimental Colonel of the 14th Light Dragoons since 1860. Charles Pinney became a Tory but decided that he had had enough of public life. A man of increasing wealth, whose wife Fanny had given him two sons, he wound up the affairs of his business in 1850 and spent his remaining years quietly living in his fine home at Camp House, Clifton

Down, regarded by his friends as amiable, genial and well-informed. He died, aged 74, on the 17th of July 1867. Another Reform Bill, which improved the system of local government, had been passed only two days before but it was to be another two generations before ordinary people got the vote and a greater say in what went on.

As to the children of the soft-hearted Irish colonel who had done his best under very difficult circumstances and had steadfastly refused to hurt his fellow men despite all their transgressions, on the 2nd of May 1837 Catherine, the eldest, died of a fever — a word used in those days to explain away the many unknown ailments. It was her birthday and she was eleven years old. Her sister Mary was sent to Cape Province in South Africa to be looked after by her mother's father, Hamilton Ross, a businessman.

Even in death Tom Brereton was not to find peace for on the night of 24th November 1940 one of many German bombs dropped on Bristol destroyed Clifton Parish church. The repair of the shattered city naturally took priority over less important matters and due to a wartime shortage of labour it was decided that the crypt in which his body had been buried would be filled in and covered over with turf.

He lies somewhere under the grass surrounded by the bones of many genteel Bristolians, at the top of a hill from which there is a long view over the city in which the rabble lived in their hovels.

*

A *Charmed* Life